Other titles in the A Retreat With... Series:

A RETREAT WITH
CATHERINE OF SIENA

Living the Truth in Love

Elizabeth A. Dreyer

ST. ANTHONY MESSENGER PRESS

Cincinnati, Ohio

Scripture citations are taken from the *New Revised Standard Version Bible*, copyright ©1989 by the Division of Christian Education of the National Council of Churches of Christ in the U.S.A., and used by permission. All rights reserved.

Excerpts from *The Prayers of Catherine of Siena*, ed. Suzanne Noffke, copyright ©1983; *The Dialogue*, by Catherine of Siena, trans. Suzanne Noffke, copyright ©1980; *Spiritualities of the Heart*, by Annice Callahan, copyright ©1990, are used by permission of Paulist Press. Excerpts from *Sayings of the Desert Fathers*, trans. Benedicta Ward, copyright ©1975, Cistercian Publications; *Mythology*, by Edith Hamilton, Little, Brown and Company, Publishers; *The Letters of St. Catherine of Siena*, trans. Suzanne Noffke, copyright ©1988, Center for Medieval and Early Rennaissance Studies, State University of New York at Binghamton; *L'Osservatore Romano*; *A Distant Mirror: The Calamitous 14th Century*, Barbara Tuchman, copyright ©1979, Random House, Inc.; *The Life of Catherine of Siena*, by Raymond of Capua, trans. Conleth Kearns, copyright ©1980, and *Catherine of Siena's Way*, by Mary Ann Fatula, copyright ©1987, by Michael Glazier; *The Practice of Faith*, copyright ©1992, and *Prayers of a Lifetime*, copyright ©1985, by Karl Rahner, The Crossroad Publishing Co., Inc., are used by permission of the publishers. The prayer on p. 44 is adapted from *Book of Worship United Church of Christ*, copyright ©1986, and used by permission of the United Church of Christ Office for Church Life and Leadership. Excerpts from *Catherine of Siena: Vision Through a Distant Eye*, by Suzanne Noffke, copyright ©1996 by The Order of St. Benedict, Inc. Published by The Liturgical Press, Collegeville, Minn. Used with permission.

Cover illustration by Steve Erspamer, S.M.
Cover and book design by Mary Alfieri
Electronic format and pagination by Sandy L. Digman

ISBN 0-86716-303-8

Copyright ©1999, Elizabeth A. Dreyer

Published by St. Anthony Messenger Press
Printed in the U.S.A.

Contents

Introducing A Retreat With...

Twenty years ago I made a weekend retreat at a
Franciscan house on the coast of New Hampshire. The
retreat director's opening talk was as lively as a long-
range weather forecast. He told us how completely God
loves each one of us—without benefit of lively anecdotes
or fresh insights.

As the friar rambled on, my inner critic kept up a
sotto voce commentary: "I've heard all this before." "Wish
he'd say something new that I could chew on." "That
poor man really doesn't have much to say." Ever hungry
for manna yet untasted, I devalued any experience of
hearing the same old thing.

After a good night's sleep, I awoke feeling as peaceful
as a traveler who has at last arrived safely home. I walked
across the room toward the closet. On the way I passed
the sink with its small framed mirror on the wall above.
Something caught my eye like an unexpected presence. I
turned, saw the reflection in the mirror and said aloud,
"No wonder he loves me!"

This involuntary affirmation stunned me. What or
whom had I seen in the mirror? When I looked again, it
was "just me," an ordinary person with a lower-than-
average reservoir of self-esteem. But I knew that in the
initial vision I had seen God-in-me breaking through like
a sudden sunrise.

At that moment I knew what it meant to be made in
the divine image. I understood right down to my size
eleven feet what it meant to be loved exactly as I was.

Only later did I connect this revelation with one granted to the Trappist monk-writer Thomas Merton. As he reports in *Conjectures of a Guilty Bystander*, while standing all unsuspecting on a street corner one day, he was overwhelmed by the "joy of being...a member of a race in which God Himself became incarnate.... There is no way of telling people that they are all walking around shining like the sun."

As an absentminded homemaker may leave a wedding ring on the kitchen windowsill, so I have often mislaid this precious conviction. But I have never forgotten that particular retreat. It persuaded me that the Spirit rushes in where it will. Not even a boring director or a judgmental retreatant can withstand the "violent wind" that "fills the entire house" where we dwell in expectation (see Acts 2:2).

So why deny ourselves any opportunity to come aside awhile and rest on holy ground? Why not withdraw from the daily web that keeps us muddled and wound? Wordsworth's complaint is ours as well: "The world is too much with us." There is no flu shot to protect us from infection by the skepticism of the media, the greed of commerce, the alienating influence of technology. We need retreats as the deer needs the running stream.

An Invitation

This book and its companions in the *A Retreat With...* series from St. Anthony Messenger Press are designed to meet that need. They are an invitation to choose as director some of the most powerful, appealing and wise mentors our faith tradition has to offer.

Our directors come from many countries, historical eras and schools of spirituality. At times they are teamed to sing in close harmony (for example, Francis de Sales, Jane de Chantal and Aelred of Rievaulx on spiritual friendship). Others are paired to kindle an illuminating fire from the friction of their differing views (such as Augustine of Hippo and Mary Magdalene on human sexuality). All have been chosen because, in their humanness and their holiness, they can help us grow in self-knowledge, discernment of God's will and maturity in the Spirit.

Inviting us into relationship with these saints and holy ones are inspired authors from today's world, women and men whose creative gifts open our windows to the Spirit's flow. As a motto for the authors of our series, we have borrowed the advice of Dom Frederick Dunne to the young Thomas Merton. Upon joining the Trappist monks, Merton wanted to sacrifice his writing activities lest they interfere with his contemplative vocation. Dom Frederick wisely advised, "Keep on writing books that make people love the spiritual life."

That is our motto. Our purpose is to foster (or strengthen) friendships between readers and retreat directors—friendships that feed the soul with wisdom, past and present. Like the scribe "trained for the kingdom of heaven," each author brings forth from his or her storeroom "what is new and what is old" (Matthew 13:52).

The Format

The pattern for each *A Retreat With...* remains the same; readers of one will be in familiar territory when they move on to the next. Each book is organized as a seven-session retreat that readers may adapt to their own schedules or to the needs of a group.

Day One begins with an anecdotal introduction called "Getting to Know Our Directors." Readers are given a telling glimpse of the guides with whom they will be sharing the retreat experience. A second section, "Placing Our Directors in Context," will enable retreatants to see the guides in their own historical, geographical, cultural and spiritual settings.

Having made the human link between seeker and guide, the authors go on to "Introducing Our Retreat Theme." This section clarifies how the guide(s) are especially suited to explore the theme and how the retreatant's spirituality can be nourished by it.

After an original "Opening Prayer" to breathe life into the day's reflection, the author, speaking with and through the mentor(s), will begin to spin out the theme. While focusing on the guide(s)' own words and experience, the author may also draw on Scripture, tradition, literature, art, music, psychology or contemporary events to illuminate the path.

Each day's session is followed by reflection questions designed to challenge, affirm and guide the reader in integrating the theme into daily life. A "Closing Prayer" brings the session full circle and provides a spark of inspiration for the reader to harbor until the next session.

Days Two through Six begin with "Coming Together in the Spirit" and follow a format similar to Day One. Day Seven weaves the entire retreat together, encourages a continuation of the mentoring relationship and concludes with "Deepening Your Acquaintance," an envoi to live the theme by God's grace, the director(s)' guidance and the retreatant's discernment. A closing section of Resources serves as a larder from which readers may draw enriching books, videos, cassettes and films.

We hope readers will experience at least one of those memorable "No wonder God loves me!" moments. And we hope that they will have "talked back" to the mentors, as good friends are wont to do.

A case in point: There was once a famous preacher who always drew a capacity crowd to the cathedral. Whenever he spoke, an eccentric old woman sat in the front pew directly beneath the pulpit. She took every opportunity to mumble complaints and contradictions— just loud enough for the preacher to catch the drift that he was not as wonderful as he was reputed to be. Others seated down front glowered at the woman and tried to shush her. But she went right on needling the preacher to her heart's content.

When the old woman died, the congregation was astounded at the depth and sincerity of the preacher's grief. Asked why he was so bereft, he responded, "Now who will help me to grow?"

All of our mentors in *A Retreat With...* are worthy guides. Yet none would seek retreatants who simply said, "Where you lead, I will follow. You're the expert." In truth, our directors provide only half the retreat's content. Readers themselves will generate the other half.

As general editor for the retreat series, I pray that readers will, by their questions, comments, doubts and decision-making, fertilize the seeds our mentors have planted.

And may the Spirit of God rush in to give the growth.

Gloria Hutchinson
Series Editor
Conversion of Saint Paul, 1995

Getting to Know Our Director

Introducing Catherine of Siena

Interest in medieval women mystics is burgeoning these days. No doubt it reflects the spiritual hunger that seems so widespread in our time and may indeed be part of what has brought us together for this retreat. Another reason may be the desire to learn more about our female ancestors in the faith. Who were these Christian women of valor and what might they teach us? Women have received short shrift in history, theology and spirituality, and we hunger to discover who they were, what they thought about, how they lived the spiritual life. Our hope is that, even though they lived a very long time ago, and by all accounts were quite extraordinary women, we might discover some common threads and meet in some shared, more ordinary space that is called the human condition.

It would be easy to look at Catherine as quite distant from our mundane existence. Most of us are not called to her life-style of penance and public witness, nor will we be remembered in posterity. We will see that Catherine was an extraordinary person! As an unlettered laywoman, she led an unusual life. And the written accounts of her life and of other fourteenth-century saints seem aimed to produce awe and wonder rather than identification. One response to their "otherness" is to dismiss them, relegate them to the trash pile of history and think no more about them. But while we must be frank about the differences between us and the saints—especially those who lived hundreds of years ago!—we are invited to join a host of Christians before us who took the time to walk with the saints and were rewarded for delving into their lives.

For even though these saints lived in a time and in a way that couldn't be more foreign to us, they continue to speak to Christians across the centuries, nudging us to think about God, to enkindle our desires, to strive to be lovers of the truth and of the world. When we take a saint like Catherine as a mentor, the point is not to follow her ideas and practices in a literal or slavish way. Rather, she invites us to open ourselves to her life with our minds and our hearts, to listen attentively to her message and, we hope, to "catch" her spirit.

Catherine Benincasa was born a twin on March 25, 1347, to Lapa di Puccio Piacenti and Jacopo Benincasa— the twenty-fourth of their twenty-five children. They lived on the Vicolo del Tiratoia in Siena. Her mother, Lapa Piacenti, was the daughter of a poet and a quilt maker and is described as having a talkative and explosive disposition.[1] She was able to nurse only one of the twins, so Catherine's sister, Giovanna, was given to a nurse. Sadly, Giovanna died in infancy, leaving Catherine as the darling of the family. In her novel about Catherine, Sigrid Undset imagines that the aging Lapa must have loved Catherine with a special, demanding and well-meaning mother-love that later made their relationship a series of heart-rending misunderstandings.[2]

Catherine's father was a prosperous dyer, endowed with a generous and calm nature. Lapa later told Catherine's biographer, Raymond of Capua, that her husband was so even-tempered and so controlled in speech that no unmeasured word ever passed his lips. Catherine's older sister, Bonaventura, recounts how hard it was for her to listen to the foul language of her husband and his friends. When his children were growing up, Jacopo had forbidden the use of bad language in the Benincasa home.

When Catherine was six, she experienced what she would later describe as a vision of Christ. Suzanne Noffke says of this experience: "After that day she became increasingly introverted and quiet, obsessively pursuing whatever her young mind and the society around her considered to be the marks of holiness. She even made a vow of virginity, since that was to the prevailing spirituality the one sure way to belong entirely to God."[3] Catherine's engagement in prayer and ascetic practices was one cause for Mama Lapa's frustration. She wanted to see Catherine happily married and a mother like herself.

But Catherine's solitary pursuits were balanced by her large family. It is not hard to imagine Catherine of Siena enmeshed in various complex webs of family and friends. Anyone who has experienced a reunion of a large family understands the complexity, the diversity, the chaos of such gatherings. They include not one, but usually several generations, ranging from the very old to the very young. And then, there may be a stray cousin or friend—like Tommaso della Fonte, who came to live with the Benincasas after he was orphaned and who, as we shall see, played an important role in Catherine's life. Each person has her or his own story, joys, successes and hurts. Each person is bound to the other through a unique history and often linked in a common future. Catherine is said to have possessed a warm, spontaneous, talkative disposition. She loved her nieces and nephews, wrote many letters, spoke often in public and confided in those closest to her.

While we may share with Catherine the experience of the complex dynamics of family life, we are less able to identify with the forces in the fourteenth century that contributed so mightily to the fragility of life. Disease, including the dreaded plague, lack of nutrition, accident and crime all made life uncertain. In 1362, Catherine's beloved sister, Bonaventura, died in childbirth. A year later, her younger sister died, and in 1368 when Catherine was 21, she lost her father. And, of course, Catherine herself died at the young age of 33. The plague struck in 1348 and 1374, in some cases wiping out a third to a half of the population in various cities across Europe.

During her short ministry, Catherine continued to live surrounded by people. She traveled with a group of favorite disciples, many of whom called her "Mama," and who saw themselves as her "family." Her prayers are laced with the phrase, "those you have given me to love with a special love." She established close and loving bonds with her spiritual directors, Tommaso della Fonte, Bartolomeo Dominici and Raymond of Capua. Tommaso della Fonte, who was taken in by the Benincasas, later became a Dominican and was Catherine's first spiritual director. She always had a special affection for him. Tommaso introduced Bartolomeo Dominici to Catherine. Bartolomeo was also a Dominican and one of the first to join Catherine's circle of friends and disciples. He, too, would later become Catherine's spiritual director and one of her closest friends. And during her work with those suffering from the plague, Catherine met the Dominican Raymond of Capua, who became the head of the Dominican order, her lifelong confidant and her biographer. Catherine was criticized for traveling freely and for keeping company with men, but she did not let such talk deter her from the mission that she felt God had entrusted to her.

The record shows that Catherine also had a forceful side to her personality. Authors comment on the frequent use of *Io voglio* (I will it) in her writings as a sign of her strong will and staunch commitment to carry out what she thought God was directing her to do. She clung to the truth, lived by the truth and sought after the truth throughout her life. She challenged the powerful and the wealthy as well as the simple. She was what we might call a "one-tracker"; that is, she did everything with drive, conviction and a refusal to compromise.

Catherine's life did not follow an ordinary path. At one point, she cut off her hair and took a vow of virginity—gestures of refusal to her parents who wanted her to marry. Catherine joined a group of Dominican laywomen called the *Mantellate* when she was about 16. This group was made up of older women, widows for the most part, who stayed in their own homes, wore a form of the Dominican habit and lived lives of prayer and service to the poor. It seems that women in late medieval Italy had several options that allowed them to live an intentional religious existence—an array of choices that some women today would like to recover. Many women took advantage of various ways to live community life— from the enclosed, canonical, cloistered convent to a number of alternative forms of religious life for laywomen who remained in the world. Some of the *Mantellate* were skeptical about admitting this much younger, volatile woman to their ranks. But, after three years of seclusion and prayer in the family home, Catherine dedicated herself to the care of the poor in her local neighborhood from 1367 to 1370.

Catherine's followers grew in number. There must have been something compelling about her person, her words and her activity that made others want to join her. Commentators use terms like vivacious, affectionate, warmth of feeling, bright, sociable, spontaneously loving to describe her. Gradually, from about the age of 25, Catherine was drawn into the public arena of both church and state. She was deeply concerned about the open conflicts among Italian city-states and between these local governments and the papacy. Often she acted as ambassador and mediator, trying to bring peace to her land and to lure Pope Gregory XI back to Rome from his outpost in Avignon. Later, in Rome, she worked hard to end the schism that resulted from the election of a second pope, Clement VII, by cardinals who were unhappy with the harsh ways of Urban VI.

Dealing with this conflict wore Catherine out. She became weak and ill, unable even to drink water. By February of 1380, she could no longer walk and was forced to stay in bed. She spent her last days with her "spiritual family." In spite of great suffering, Catherine offered them spiritual counsel, encouraging them to free themselves from clinging attachments, to trust in God's care for them and, above all, to love one another. To the last, she was giving directions and encouragement to each of her followers, both those present and those at a distance. Finally, she asked their pardon for any offenses she may have committed against them. On April 29, 1380, she died in the arms of her good friend, Alessa, with her followers around her.

Catherine was canonized in 1461 by Pope Pius II, proclaimed co-patron of Italy with Francis of Assisi in 1939 by Pope Pius XII, and declared Doctor of the Church in 1970 by Pope Paul VI, an honor held by only two other women, Teresa of Jesus (of Avila) and Thérèse of the Child Jesus of Lisieux (the Little Flower).

Catherine shares with several other medieval women mystics in England and the Low Countries the distinction of being the first woman to be published in the vernacular—in Catherine's case, in her local Italian dialect. Her written legacy can be grouped under three headings, all of which will be used as the backdrop for this retreat. The first is her major theological work, *The Dialogue of Divine Providence*, written between 1377 and 1378 when she was immersed in the work of her ministry. The second grouping contains her twenty-six prayers recorded by friends while Catherine was lost in ecstasy. Most of these prayers date from the last seventeen months of her life. The third category of writings is her letters, written throughout her lifetime to many different kinds of people and numbering 382.

Placing Our Director in Context

Catherine of Siena's World

We begin by reminding ourselves that medieval women were quite different from us. Some of their attitudes and practices, their language and imagery is foreign indeed! And the social, ecclesial, intellectual and cultural world of the Middle Ages has little in common with the world of the twenty-first century. For example, medieval attitudes regarding the body and matter reflected the dualism of Christianity's meeting with Greek philosophy in the early years of the Church. While it is certainly true that the struggle to look upon our bodies and matter as intrinsically good is far from over, we are different from medieval people in the ways we value embodiedness and the material universe as sacred gifts of God, made holy by the incarnation—an event in which matter and divine spirit are wedded in an intimate embrace. In addition, while we still struggle with temptations of every stripe, we are not likely to throw ourselves into freezing water, flagellate ourselves until the blood flows, fast until we are skin and bones or consume cancerous liquids or lice! And the education and roles that women take for granted today were off-limits for the majority of medieval women. Thus, every spirituality must be examined and practiced with a keen eye to its context. What made eminent sense in the fourteenth century in Italy, may make little sense today.

However, when we meet these women, we do discover some common threads. They were very interested in the human, rather than the divine, Jesus. They encountered Jesus as a tender lover, an unselfish giver, as one whose love led to incredible suffering on the cross—suffering that was graphically described in texts and portrayed in art. They also struggled with themselves, with their roles in society and Church, with lack of self-confidence, with feelings of depression and sadness. They were women of passion and desire, women who mustered their strength and courage to love the Lord in both extraordinary and quite ordinary ways. They worked hard, prayed hard, took risks and remained committed, even in the face of great obstacles.

Suzanne Noffke describes the fourteenth century as a time of crises and turning points for Church and society.[4] Most portraits of the time are painted with very dark, calamitous and foreboding strokes. In one of the most widely read books on the fourteenth century, *A Distant Mirror*, Barbara Tuchman sees it as a mirror of our own. She calls it a "violent, tormented, bewildered, suffering and disintegrating age." She also says it "suffered so many 'strange and great perils and adversities'...that its disorders cannot be traced to any one cause...plague, war, taxes, brigandage, bad government, insurrection [or] schism in the Church."[5] Another historian produces these phrases, descriptive of the time: economic chaos, social unrest, high prices, profiteering, depraved morals, lack of production, industrial indolence, frenetic gaiety, wild expenditure, luxury, debauchery, social and religious hysteria, greed, maladministration, decay of manners. An eyewitness of the fourteenth century captures the misery in a poem:

> Time of mourning and temptation,
> > Age of envy, torment, tears,
> Time of languor and damnation
> > Age of last declining years,
> Time of falseness, full of horror,
> > Age of lying, envy, strife,
> Time without true judgment, honor,
> > Age of sadness, shortening life.[6]

But we must remember that history is complex and that there is always a "normal" side to life, even in the harshest of times. Catherine and her family suffered from this chaos, but they also escaped some of the worst of it because of their wealth and position.

Perhaps the greatest scourge of the century was the Black Death. Brought to Italy on ships from the East, this frightening disease was at its most virulent between 1348 and 1350. Imagine what it would be like if a third of the population of New York City were to be wiped out in a short time. The sickness was no respecter of persons— rich, middle-class, poor, men, women, children succumbed to its power. Businesses were abandoned, wealthy estates left vacant, basic services interrupted. And there was also the psychological toll on those who survived. Robbers and marauders had a field day. Civilized ways of doing business were compromised. Many people lost the will to continue to live, and hope and work for a better tomorrow.

On the civic front, Italy was racked by tensions and violent confrontations. Powerful dukes, desiring to extend control over north and central Italy, sent armies to capture new land. After 1350, many of the great banking houses of Italy went bankrupt, largely caused by the default of

their chief debtor, Edward III of England. In the summer
of 1373, a bad harvest in Tuscany resulted in famine. The
newly emerging professional guilds fought with each
other for power and wealth. The lower classes rioted and
went on destructive rampages. Merchants lived with the
daily uncertainty of war, pestilence, famine and
insurrection. The labor shortage caused by the plague
revived the demand for slaves. By the end of the
fourteenth century, there was hardly a well-to-do
household in Tuscany without at least one slave.

Some Italian cities fought not only among themselves
but against the papacy as well. There was constant strife
between the merchant Guelphs, who supported the
papacy, and the aristocratic Ghibellines, who stood with
the empire. Florence was at the center of this controversy,
and Catherine was early drawn into it as mediator and
peacemaker. Florence created an emergency government
of eight, got most of the central Italian cities to join them,
expelled papal vicars and declared war on Gregory XI.

The pope responded with an interdict in 1376. He
called the Florentines heretics and ordered all Christian
rulers to expel Florentine merchants and confiscate their
property. It is hard for us to imagine a pope announcing
publicly that God would not be offended if one were to
rob Florentine merchants! Of course, this only made the
merchants more resentful of what they perceived as the
greed and arrogance of high Church prelates.

When Catherine went to Florence in the spring of
1378 to negotiate peace on behalf of Gregory XI, members
of the lower classes rioted, brutally attacking several
wealthy Guelph families. Raymond of Capua writes that
when Catherine suggested that some of Florence's leaders
who were against peace with the papacy be deprived of
their offices, this information was circulated to the
"ignorant rabble in the streets," who "cried out 'Let us

capture her and burn her, this most wicked woman! or put her to the sword.'" Her host threw them all out for fear of having his house burned to the ground. She and her companions went to a garden to pray. Soon the rioters arrived with swords and clubs, shouting, "Where is that wicked woman? Where is she?"[7] Mary Ann Fatula writes of the incident, "As the assassin drew near, Catherine's joy and courage at the thought of martyrdom disarmed him; he turned away, leaving her to weep at the dream that had slipped from her hands."[8]

Things within the Church were not much better. The pope had taken up residence in Avignon, France, and was deeply enmeshed in the power structures of the French monarchy. Catherine traveled to Avignon, and worked tirelessly to convince the pope to return to Rome. The papacy also suffered from its conflict with Florence and other central Italian cities. In 1378, Gregory XI died and Urban VI was elected. The new pope's desire for reform took a tyrannical turn. The French cardinals protested by declaring his election invalid and naming instead the ruthless cardinal of Geneva, who took the name Clement VII. Urban asked for Catherine, and in November of 1378, she traveled to Rome with twenty-four of her disciples. But in the end, Catherine saw her efforts as useless. The forces of disunity and violent antagonism weakened both her body and spirit, leading to her death in Rome on April 29, 1380.

In the midst of all this chaos and uncertainty, there arose in Italy a number of saints, many of them women who had conversions in early life. Some were, like Catherine, linked to the third orders. One well-known Franciscan is Angela of Foligno. Others became involved in the social and ecclesial struggles of their time. Birgitta of Sweden spent many years in Rome, fighting against some of the same abuses that engaged Catherine.

Germany claims Meister Eckhart, Henry Suso and Johannes Tauler. England also enjoyed a flowering of mysticism in the persons of Julian of Norwich, Walter Hilton, Margery Kempe and Richard Rolle.

In our retreat, we will walk with Catherine and hear her invitation to us to share in her intense passion for the truth. We will meet the God whom she called "Gentle Truth"; struggle with the sin and glory of our own truth; ponder the fruits of truth—discernment, freedom and wisdom.

> And in love
> you drew us out of yourself,
> giving us being
> in your own image and likeness.
> You eternal Truth,
> have told me the truth:
> that love compelled you to create us.[9]

Notes

[1] Mary Ann Fatula, *Catherine of Siena's Way* (Wilmington, Del.: Michael Glazier, 1987), p. 24.

[2] Sigrid Undset, *Catherine of Siena* (New York: Sheed and Ward, 1954), p. 14.

[3] Suzanne Noffke, *Catherine of Siena: Vision Through a Distant Eye* (Collegeville, Minn.: The Liturgical Press, 1996), pp. 1-2.

[4] Noffke, p. 7.

[5] Barbara Tuchman, *A Distant Mirror: The Calamitous 14th Century* (New York: Ballantine Books, 1978), p. xiii.

[6] Eustashe Deschamps, cited in Ellen Murray, "Tears: Symbol of Conversion in the Writings of Catherine of Siena" (doctoral dissertation, St. Louis University, 1996), p. 1.

[7] Raymond of Capua, *The Life of Catherine of Siena*, trans. Conleth Kearns (Wilmington, Del.: Michael Glazier, 1980), p. 385.

[8] Fatula, p. 35.

[9] *The Prayers of Catherine of Siena*, ed. Suzanne Noffke (Mahwah, N.J.: Paulist Press, 1983).

DAY ONE

'I Am the Way, and the Truth, and the Life' (JOHN 14:6)

Introducing Our Retreat Theme

Thomas Merton reminds us that the truth we ultimately seek as Christians is not a philosopher's abstraction, but God's very self.[1] The mystics invite us to open ourselves to the Holy Spirit who enables us to see and appreciate the full reality of the truths contained in hitherto "untasted" conceptual statements about God. Contemplative experience is always an experience of God who is encountered, not as an abstraction nor as a distant, alien Being, but as intimately and immediately present to us in infinite Reality and Essence.[2] This retreat is an opportunity to pause and encounter the God who is Truth and reflect on what it means for each of us to love and live in the truth.

We do know that the term *truth* had special meaning for Catherine of Siena. Her affection for this term certainly stemmed from her affiliation with the Dominican order. As a child growing up in Siena, she lived but a stone's throw from the Dominican church, San Domenico. The friars, clothed in their black and white habits, would have been a familiar sight as they walked along her street, celebrated the liturgies Catherine attended and preached from the storehouse of Dominican theology, including that of Thomas Aquinas.

The motto of the Dominican order is "to contemplate and to give to others the fruit of that contemplation" (*contemplare et aliis tradere contemplata*). Some of us may be new to the experience of contemplation; others may be old hands at it. But in either case, as laypeople, we may be timid about the next step—the responsibility to share with others the fruit of that prayer in word and act. It is not enough just to walk the way of the gospel privately. We are also called to entrust the fruit of our encounters with God to others. Catherine's choice to become a lay Dominican suggests that she wanted to bring that word of truth to the broader world. This outreach to the world allows us to feel a greater kinship with Catherine. She called Saint Dominic, the founder of the order, "an apostle in the world," a title that fits Catherine as well—and one to which we should all aspire!

Catherine's letters are a gold mine, revealing her loving concern, her common sense, her willingness to prod others to live virtuous lives. She sent letters of encouragement and chastisement to disciples, friends, princes and popes. Catherine shows us how to use our particular gifts to spread the good news of the truth to others and to the suffering in the world. We may be letter writers; we may speak the truth in our family and business affairs; we may express the truth through art or music; we may speak the truth to a friend over coffee; or we may witness to the truth in action for justice. Catherine would be the first to celebrate each person's unique path to discern and preach the truth.

At the source of her passion for truth was the God she delighted in addressing as "Eternal Truth" or "First Gentle Truth." Surely Catherine can teach us something about how to touch the truth of our own lives, how to face up to and confront the illusions and defenses that prevent us from seeing the truth about ourselves, our families, our world and God. Let our prayer be not only to speak the truth, but to hear it, live it, embrace it.

Opening Prayer

O all-powerful, eternal God,
O boundless most gentle charity!
I see in you and know in my heart
that you are the way, the truth, and life
by which everyone must travel
who is destined to come to you—
the way, the truth, and life
which your unutterable love establishes and fashions
out of the true knowledge of the wisdom
of your only begotten Son, our Lord Jesus Christ.
You are the eternal and incomprehensible God
who, when the human race was dead
because of our wretched weakness,
were moved only by love
and by merciful compassion
to send us this one,
our true God and Lord,
Christ Jesus your Son,
clothed in our mortal flesh.[3]

RETREAT SESSION ONE

In the Greek world into which Christianity moved in its early years, philosophers used the imagery of light to speak about truth. The sense organ linked to the truth was the eye. To live in the truth meant that one was able to "see." Christianity appropriated and transformed this

imagery, employing it to speak about the truth of God
and the truth in human persons. In her writings,
Catherine favors the biblical thought of Paul and John the
Evangelist. John's Gospel features light imagery in a
prominent way:

> And this is the judgment, that the light has come
> into the world, and people loved darkness rather
> than light because their deeds were evil. For all who
> do evil hate the light and do not come to the light,
> so that their deeds may not be exposed. But those
> who do what is true come to the light, so that it may
> be clearly seen that their deeds have been done in
> God.[4]

Catherine takes this tradition and reworks it in her own
key. She prays:

> Eternal Godhead!
> O high eternal Godhead!
> Boundless love!
> In your light I have seen light;
> in your light I have come to know the light;
> in your light
> we come to know the source of light
> and the source of darkness—
> that you are the source of all light,
> and we the source of darkness.
> . . .
>
> And your Truth reveals as well
> the means by which we come to know the light,
> the garment of your gentle will.
> What a marvelous thing,
> that even while we are in the dark
> we should know the light![5]

When we are in the darkness of selfishness or depression,
it seems as though the light of God's tender touch will
never reach us. Catherine's encounter with God produced

a trust and a conviction that we can know the light even when we are in the midst of hard times. The truth of our existence is that we remain always in God's loving sight, no matter how dark our life becomes at times. It is an illusion, she says, to think that God does not care for us or that we are beyond the pale of God's extended hand. Catherine herself often encountered hard times. She was finely attuned to the darkness in herself and in those around her. And yet she pleads with her readers to persevere, to trust that the power of God's love is more powerful than our penchant for evil. She invites us to trust that *in the very midst of our darkness* the light remains and will lead us out into the sunlight of God's love.

In our present era of psychology, we make distinctions that would have been foreign to the Middle Ages. We may note the difference between good and bad darkness or be more attuned to the positive role of the darkness at different points in our psychic development. Feminist writers talk about the sheltering, germinating functions of the dark—processes that are crucial to a full and "bright" life. In contrast, Catherine usually uses the term *darkness* to refer to sinfulness. It describes our penchant toward self-centeredness, evil and falsehood. Darkness describes the choice to give in to despair, cynicism and deceit. Light points to their opposites.

The fire that produces light is also the fire that produces heat. Many mystics use passionate, erotic images to speak of their relationship with God. But Catherine, more than others, portrays God as one who is madly in love with creatures. One of her prayers expresses this theme repeatedly:

Thanks,
thanks to you,
most high eternal Father,
for showing us today—

madly in love as you are with your creature—
... how your bride, holy church,
can be reformed.[6]

... O you who are madly in love with your creature[7]

... O eternal Trinity, mad with love[8]

She asks what drove God to offer God's self as our food
and then answers her own question: "What drove you?
Nothing but your charity, mad with love as you are!"[9]

And in *The Dialogue* she writes, "O mad lover! It was
not enough for you to take our humanity: you had to die
as well!"[10]

This kind of language takes us by surprise. How often
do we think of God as one who is madly in love with us?
For Catherine, God is "like one drunk with love for our
good." By showing us the love in which we were created,
God fires up an even greater love and sorrow within us.[11]

The truth that Catherine wants us to discover is God's
goodness toward us, for once we know this truth, love
will follow. The way to "savor and be enlightened by this
truth" is through continual humble prayer that is
grounded in the truth of God and the truth of ourselves.
Through prayer, we are united with God and follow in
the footsteps of Christ crucified. Through desire and
affection and the union of love, God makes of us another
God's self. The truth, according to Catherine, is that by
love's affection the soul becomes another God.[12]

Our task then, is to get in touch with our love's
affection. Where in our lives do we experience tenderness
toward another? Where does our heart burn and reach
out to others? Where are we filled with the warmth of
genuine love? To what does our desire reach out? For
what do we yearn?

After we reflect on these human affections, we can
ask about our relationship with God. Does God seem real

enough for us to experience this kind of affection? Do we honestly *want* God, and if so, what specific contours does this desire take? Do we link our affections for other people to our relationship with God? Catherine invites us to rekindle the fire of our desires and to discover the truth about God's mad love for us. We can outline the various truths about God that have come down to us in the Scriptures and Tradition, but it is only when we have fallen in love with God that the truth of God really becomes visible—when we are in God and God is in us like the "fish is in the sea and the sea is in the fish."[13] What followed from this love for Catherine was her will to know and follow truth more courageously.[14]

But in Catherine's Christological outlook, the most visible and compelling truth about God is Jesus, the Christ. In *The Dialogue*, Catherine develops at great length the image of Christ as the bridge. Dominican priest and scholar Benedict Ashley suggests that Catherine imagines the bridge to be one of those covered bridges seen in Tuscan cities, a bridge that has little shops and taverns on either side of a main thoroughfare. In Catherine's hands, the bridge becomes "a multivalent, allegorical parable for the doctrine of the Incarnation."[15] Adam's sin caused a separation between God and humanity that can only be bridged by the incarnate Truth, Jesus Christ. Christians must take three steps—signifying stages of the spiritual life—that will bring them across the bridge of Christ from his feet to his heart to his mouth, leading eventually to the Father.

At the first step, we obey Christ out of fear rather than love. At the second step, we act out of love, but a love that is still tinged with selfishness because we lack perfect understanding. At the third step, Christ speaks the truth and claims his bride with a nuptial kiss.[16] The way of truth is the way of Christ, and Catherine warns her readers to take heed that they not take the path *beneath* the bridge—the waters below are raging and treacherous—for it is not the way of truth.[17]

For Catherine, the only way to knowledge of the truth is Christ's blood. Christ's way of truth culminates in the cross. In *The Dialogue*, Catherine asks Christ why he wanted his side pierced when he was already dead. Christ responds that there were many reasons, but the chief reason was that while his longing for humankind was infinite, the actual deed of bearing pain was finite and could never show the depth of his love. "This is why I wanted you to see the secret of my heart, wanted to show it to you opened up, so that you would see that I loved you more than finite suffering could show."[18]

The invitation to contemplate the open heart of Christ leads to a deeper understanding of the way in which God relates to us. Many medieval women mystics speak of experiencing God in a very physical way. They speak of nursing at Christ's breasts, of intimate encounters and kisses, of being invited to enter into the very body of Christ through his wounds and heart. Their knowledge of God's infinite love does not arise from a cerebral experience. They use very earthy, tactile images to speak of their "spiritual" experiences of God. This knowledge of God's endless, passionate love leads us to the truth about ourselves, allowing us to shed the cloud of selfish love and find the way.[19]

People like Catherine experienced God in an enveloping way, allowing them to feel and touch the enormity of these words in John's Gospel: "And the Word became flesh and lived among us, and we have seen his glory, the glory as of a father's only son, full of grace and truth.... From his fullness we have all received, grace upon grace. The law indeed was given through Moses; grace and truth came through Jesus Christ."[20]

For Catherine, contemplation on the Incarnation allows us to plumb the depths of God's true reality. In one of her letters, she notes that in the heart of Christ, we "discover hearty love, for all that Christ does in us he does, as this shows, with that sort of hearty love."[21] Catherine used a lot of "heart talk." Her expression *hearty love* makes one think of the term *hearty soup*, which is opposed to a weak, watery, less nutritious version. Catherine wants to convince us that God's love is the "hearty" variety and until we encounter this love, we will not see the truth of who God really is.

In another letter to Frate Bartolomeo Dominici, Catherine describes this love as hunger:

> Oh Jesus, gentlest love! You have said, "Do you want an incentive to work for my glory and other people's salvation? Do you want the strength to endure every trial with patience? Then look at me, the Lamb slain on the cross for you, my blood totally drained from head to foot. I pay no attention to your foolishness, nor does your ingratitude deter me from working out your salvation. I am like one crazed and transformed by my hunger for you. [22]

For Catherine, another truth about God's love is that God is hungry for us. And just as God hungers for us, we, too, are to hunger for souls. Catherine's readers may be struck by the oddness of her constant reference to "being hungry for, and eating souls." But for her, our love of others leads to hunger for their souls, and this is part of our truth because we live in "Gentle Truth."

The richness of her imagery and metaphors nudges our imaginations to delve into who the Truth of God is for us. Catherine gives us a glimpse of the many and various ways in which she spoke about the Truth who is God. She invites us to delve into our own reservoirs. She does not want us to be satisfied with a heady, abstract idea of truth. No, she wants us to put flesh and blood and feeling into our ideas about what is true and who is true. Along with Catherine, we set out on our own quest for Truth—in God, in ourselves and in our world.

> We are able to open ourselves to a loving encounter with God because Jesus dwells with us.
> We can muster the courage to let the light of truth shine on ourselves and on our world because Jesus dwells with us.
> We can discern good from evil and choose the good because Jesus dwells with us.
> We can live with the freedom of the children of God because Jesus dwells with us.

For Reflection

- *Take a moment to think about the images you use for God. Do you ever think of God as Truth? Take a moment to ponder the God whose name is Truth. What did you discover? What blocks did you encounter?*

- *When you hear someone say, "She is true-blue," what do you think it says about the person? Do you ever think of God in this way?*

- *If God is "Truth," how might this affect the way you pray? the way you speak? the way you live?*

- *Name one or two qualities that you cherish as the most true things about yourself. Do you see these things as a participation in the Truth who is God?*

Closing Prayer

To you, O LORD, I lift up my soul.
O my God, in you I trust;
do not let me be put to shame;
do not let my enemies exult over me.

. . .

Make me to know your ways,
O LORD, teach me your paths.
Lead me in your truth, and teach me,
for you are the God of my salvation;
for you I wait all day long.[23]

"Do not let your hearts be troubled. Believe in God,
believe also in me. In my Father's house there are
many dwelling places. If it were not so, would I
have told you that I go to prepare a place for you?
And if I go and prepare a place for you, I will come
again and will take you to myself, so that where I
am, there you may be also. And you know the way
to the place where I am going." Thomas said to him,
"Lord, we do not know where you are going. How
can we know the way?" Jesus said to him, "I am the
way, and the truth, and the life. No one comes to the
Father except through me. If you know me, you will
know my Father also. From now on you do know
him and have seen him."[24]

Notes

[1] Thomas Merton, *The Ascent to Truth* (New York: Harcourt, Brace and Company, 1951), p. 10.

[2] Merton, p. 17.

[3] *Prayers*, p. 34.

[4] John 19-21.

[5] *Prayers*, p. 87.

[6] *Prayers*, p. 80.

[7] *Prayers*, pp. 78, 80.

[8] *Prayers*, p. 78.

[9] *Prayers*, p. 79

[10] Catherine of Siena, *The Dialogue*, trans. Suzanne Noffke (New York: Paulist Press, 1980).

[11] *Dialogue*, p. 55.

[12] *Dialogue*, pp. 25-26.

[13] *Dialogue*, p. 27.

[14] *Dialogue*, p. 26.

[15] Benedict Ashley, "Guide to Saint Catherine's Dialogue," *Cross and Crown* 29 (1977), p. 242.

[16] Ashley, p. 242.

[17] *The Letters of St. Catherine of Siena*, Vol. 1, trans. Suzanne Noffke (Binghamton, N.Y.: Center for Medieval and Early Renaissance Studies, State University of New York at Binghamton, 1988), Letter 272 to Raymond of Capua.

[18] *Dialogue*, p. 138.

[19] *Dialogue*, p. 30.

[20] John 1:14, 16-17.

[21] Suzanne Noffke, "Catherine of Siena: The Responsive Heart," in Annice Callahan, *Spiritualities of the Heart* (Mahwah, N.J.: Paulist Press, 1990), p. 67.

[22] *Letters*, p. 83.

[23] Psalm 25: 1-2; 4-6.

[24] John 14:1-7.

DAY TWO
Self-Knowledge: We Are Creatures and Sinners

Coming Together in the Spirit

Most of us remember the story from Greek mythology in which a handsome lad named Narcissus refused to have his head turned by all the lovely maidens who longed for his affection. Finally, one of those he had offended prayed this prayer: "May he who loves not others love himself." The great goddess Nemesis (which means *righteous anger*) heard the prayer. One day, as Narcissus bent over a clear pool of water for a drink, he saw his own reflection and immediately fell in love with it. "Now I know," he cried, "what others have suffered from me, for I burn with love of my own self—and yet how can I reach that loveliness I see mirrored in the water? But I cannot leave it. Only death can set me free." And so he pined away, leaning perpetually over the pool until finally, he died.[1]

This age-old story is reflected again in our day in a book entitled *The Culture of Narcissism* by Christopher Lasch. Lasch extrapolates from the psychological dimensions of narcissism in individuals to describe the qualities of a narcissistic society. These include dependence on warmth provided by others, fear of dependence, a sense of inner emptiness, and pseudo self-insight. Lasch suggests that we are a culture riddled with anxiety, against which we defend ourselves by living only for the present moment, that is, we live for ourselves, not for predecessors or posterity.[2]

While Catherine could not turn to Freud to understand the human psyche, she was certainly no stranger to the lure of selfishness. She cautions her readers over and over again that the great enemy of the spiritual life is self-preoccupation. She writes, "Every scandal, hatred, cruelty, and everything unbecoming springs from this root of selfish love."[3] Terms like "selfish self-centeredness," "selfish sensuality," "self-complacency" and "self-opinionatedness" pepper her texts.[4] No century has a monopoly on egoism, and Catherine invites us to come to terms with our own.

Defining Our Thematic Context

In our first session, we reflected on and set out to meet the God who is Truth. We explored the various dimensions of this God as Catherine might have understood them and realized how, for her, Truth was no abstract term but rather the name of the One who loved her madly. We noted the way in which the metaphor of light is often used by Christians to speak of the God who is Truth. Just like people who speak the truth, God is one who can be relied on, one we can trust and from whom we can draw confidence.

On this second day of retreat, we reflect on the human condition as the great contrast with the reality of God. We delve into a most basic truth about ourselves— that we are creatures, not the Creator; sinners, not the sinless One.

Opening Prayer

Ineffable Creator,

. . .

You are proclaimed
>
> the true font of light and wisdom
> and the primal origin
> raised beyond all things.

Pour forth a ray of Your brightness
>
> into the darkened places of my mind;
> disperse from my soul
> the twofold darkness
> into which I was born:
> sin and ignorance.

You make eloquent the tongues of infants.
>
> Refine my speech
> and pour forth upon my lips
> the goodness of Your blessing.

Grant to me
>
> keenness of mind,
> capacity to remember,
> skill in learning,
> subtlety to interpret,
> and eloquence of speech.

May You
>
> guide the beginning of my work,
> direct its progress,
> and bring it to completion.

You Who are true God and true Man,
>
> Who live and reign, world without end.
> Amen.[5]

Retreat Session Two

Catherine's works are full of references to self-knowledge and knowledge of God. Often she places both phrases in the same sentence, since she sees them as intimately related to each other. Perhaps because she spent three years in solitary prayer in her room in her parents' home, she often refers to the "cell" or the "house" of self-knowledge. She may also have felt compelled to emphasize the "cell within" to counter her critics, who would have preferred to have her in her cell than traveling about Europe, conversing with popes and princes. In a letter to her first spiritual director, Tommaso della Fonte, she describes the "cell of the soul" as a well in which there is both earth [our poverty] and living water [the very core of the knowledge of God's will that we be made holy].[6] One comes to know oneself by turning inward in quiet reflection. She encourages us to enter into the depths of this well, into loving transformation.

Like Catherine, we, too, gain self-knowledge by inner reflection and honest self-assessment. But in our age of psychological awareness, we also name the ways in which self-knowledge comes to us from others. We see that growth in true self-knowledge is aided by others who are close to us and who can reflect to us truths about ourselves that we may not otherwise notice. These insights may involve our faults—reminding us that we *are* sinners. But it may also point to gifts and beauties—reminding us that we are *also* made in God's image—a theme to which we will return on Day Four.

Catherine uses her famous, dramatic juxtaposition of opposites to speak about God in relationship to humans. She prays,

You, eternal Godhead,
are life
and I am death.
You are wisdom
and I am ignorance.
You are light
and I am darkness.
You are infinite
and I am finite.
You are absolute directness
and I am terrible twistedness.
You are the doctor
and I am sick.[7]

Such a powerful statement of how we are *not* like God!
Catherine wants us to come to terms with the shadow
side of our existence. In order to force us to confront our
sinfulness with honesty and courage, she employs a
rather dramatic metaphor. She compares sin to leprosy.[8]
Adam's sin, she says, oozed with a deadly pus, until the
incarnation effected a cure, draining the pus out of
Adam's sin, leaving only its scar.[9] No doubt this imagery
was impressed on Catherine's mind as she went about
nursing those who suffered from plague and other
diseases.

This language may grate on modern ears. Theology
and spirituality today focus not on God's distance, but on
God's nearness to us. We are more comfortable with the
God within than with the God who is the awesome
Creator of the universe. And it is certainly hard for a
culture that puts so much energy into human
development and psychological awareness to hear words
like "I am death" or "I am ignorance." How are we to
understand these words of Catherine? Do they have a
message for us in spite of their seeming dissonance? We
can examine the truth of our sinfulness in the context of
another of Catherine's favorite themes: self-knowledge.

So many mystics begin their discussions of the spiritual life by underlining the importance of self-knowledge that I have begun to call self-knowledge the "first base" of the spiritual life. In our psychological age, most of us take it for granted that self-knowledge is an important part of the development of a mature individual. Rows and rows of self-help books line the shelves in our bookstores. Psychological tools like the enneagram and the Myers-Briggs inventory teach us about how different personality types function; they help us to understand more deeply what motivates our behavior and respond more accurately to others whose patterns may be different from ours. In our post-Freudian culture, the desire for psychological insight into self has become as common as running water and electricity. As with any intellectual or cultural development, we need to guard against abuse, to make sure that our use of these aids does not nurture an ego trip.

Medieval mystics like Catherine, living hundreds of years before Freud and Jung, take a different slant when they speak of self-knowledge. And it is challenging for us moderns to understand their words without a psychological overlay. But we must try. We can ask, what do they *mean* when they use the term *self-knowledge*? For Catherine, self-knowledge is the cell or dwelling in which we discover our own lowliness that makes us humble. Three important elements are contained in this statement. First, the context for knowledge of our sinfulness is Catherine's encounter with a God who is infinite, blazing charity. Second, it is simply the truth that we are the creature—not the Creator—and that we are sinful. This is not intended as a put-down to undermine our self-assurance. It is simply the truth. Third, this experience, when it is genuine, produces the fruit of humility in our hearts. When I see the truth of my own smallness and ingratitude compared to God's utter gracious magnanimity, there is not much to brag about. This particular experience is foundational, but it is not the whole story. Later we will reflect on our being as a place that also reveals God's goodness, and in this light a warm fire of love is born in us. In this fire, bitterness turns to sweetness, weakness becomes strength and the ice of selfish love melts away. When we encounter the truth of ourselves, we are then able to love ourselves, our neighbor and God for God and not for our own selfish ends.[10]

In response to Catherine's request to know and love God, the supreme Truth, God says to her, "Here is the way, if you would come to perfect knowledge and enjoyment of me, eternal Life: Never leave the knowledge of yourself. Then, put down as you are in the valley of humility you will know me in yourself, and from this knowledge you will draw all that you need.... You will find humility in the knowledge of yourself when you see that even your own existence comes not from yourself but from me, for I loved you before you came into being. And in my unspeakable love for you I willed to create you anew in grace. So I washed you and made you a new creation in the blood that my only-begotten Son poured out with such burning love."[11] Catherine links lack of knowledge with evil. When we don't get the picture right, we fall into sin.[12]

Catherine is not the only mystic to teach this truth. Teresa of Jesus, a Spanish mystic who lived in the sixteenth century, has a similar message. The truth of human beings is threefold. First, she says we are creatures, not the Creator. Second, we are sinners. And third, we are made in the image and likeness of God. In this session, we focus on the knowledge of our lowliness and sinfulness. In session four, we will explore the presence of God's goodness within us, the truth that we are *imago dei*—made in the image and likeness of God.

When Catherine and Teresa call attention to our creatureliness and sinful inclinations, they are not laying a guilt trip on anybody. Nor would they have a clue about our fear that talk about sin drags us down or diminishes us. For a medieval person, sin was simply a truth of life. "If we say that we have no sin, we deceive ourselves, and the truth is not in us."[13] These mystics write about self-knowledge in order to help others set out on the journey to God, and they want their readers to "get the picture straight" before they embark, if they want to avoid disaster. If we don't begin in the truth, the journey is bound to have an unhappy ending. It is as simple and straightforward as that.

Today, some theologians link self-knowledge with the work of the Holy Spirit. The Spirit teaches us who we are, always in the context of relationship. Just as Jesus was led by the Spirit to a growing self-awareness and self-identity vis-à-vis the Father, we, too, can open ourselves to the Spirit's prompting to help us come into a true possession of ourselves, undistorted by sin. In tandem, our relationships with others and with God lead us to the truth of who we are. A key aspect of our identity is that we are loved by God. Gradually the Spirit works in us to make us wholly new, and we begin to see things from God's perspective, to choose continuously to live in the truth of our existence. "The joy of the Kingdom belongs to those to whom it has been given to inhale the truth about themselves."[14] Catherine was deeply aware of both poles of our true self-identity.

Catherine's insistence on self-knowledge bears the mark of her intense personality. Nowhere is this more visible than in her awareness of her own sinfulness. In her *Prayers*, she is constantly juxtaposing her sinfulness and the sinfulness of the world with God's loving mercy. The phrase, "I have sinned against the Lord; have mercy on me!" runs like a leitmotif throughout. In a letter to two of her friends, Catherine writes, "I, Caterina, a useless servant, am in agony with desire as I search the depths of my soul; I grieve and weep when I see and really understand our foolish apathy, our failure to give our love to God after God has given us such great graces with so much love."[15]

How might we account for this deep sense of sin? To begin, we might point to Catherine's prophetic side. Prophets are usually people who have a very delicate and sensitive awareness of evil. Even the smallest transgression looms large in their eyes. Prophets are very tuned in to the wrongs of the world. They empathize with the oppressed, with those who suffer injustice, and they cry out and rage against those who perpetrate it.

We have also seen that Catherine lived in a time of great violence and upheaval. In the fourteenth century, she was confronted daily with greed, contention, war and deception in Church and society. We too, in this century, have witnessed horrors of human cruelty, leading us to ask about our complicity and silence in the face of evil. Catherine not only acknowledged her own sin but asked that the sin of the world be placed on her shoulders as well. She called those around her to a grown-up kind of accountability. She was a great advocate of human freedom. One is always free to choose virtue or sin. No one, she said, not even the devil, can force us to sin unless we cooperate.[16]

But above all, Catherine's sharp awareness of sin was grounded in her vision of God. The God she met was a God of such incredible love that even the slightest affront was unbearable. How can we turn our backs on a God who professes to be madly in love with us? When egotistic preoccupations hold center stage in our relationships with God and others, acknowledgment of sin feels like an embarrassment. We may feel like we got "caught red-handed." We feel bad, not because we have offended someone or transgressed the law, but because we have fallen down in our own image of ourselves. We are forced to admit that we are not as perfect as we pretended to be.

The resulting guilt produces sadness and, at times, paralysis. We lose interest in doing good. On the other hand, when the love of God and others is at the center of our lives, sin produces the opposite effect. We are devastated that we have betrayed someone who loves us so much. The effect of this kind of acknowledgment of sin is not guilt, but deep sorrow. This sorrow leads to asking for forgiveness and when reconciliation takes place, one is filled with joy to be "back in covenant" with the beloved. Energy returns and one resolves to be a better lover in the future. This latter experience is what comes through in Catherine's text. She invites us to exchange leprosy for brightness on the face of our souls.

We can also reflect on times when we actually felt awe, when we were overwhelmed by the power or the beauty of reality. At such times, we can feel puny and insignificant, dwarfed by the scale of the universe or the depth of someone's love. When we hold an ice floe calved from an Alaskan glacier, or gaze on a rock and contemplate the age of the universe—our short span of life seems like nothing in light of the millions and millions of years these works of nature have been in existence!

Or when we marvel at the perfect formation of human features on a newborn child—it is *this* kind of experience that gives rise to an awareness of what Catherine calls humility or ingratitude. In these moments, we stand stupefied, thunderstruck, wowed at the immensity of God and at our own comparable nothingness. The saints are people who manage to develop and maintain such dispositions throughout their lives. Their encounters with God are such that this sense of themselves as insignificant creatures and sinners becomes like the daily air they breathe. It is the truth of who they are because they have encountered the truth of who God is.

For Reflection

- *Recall an intimate relationship when you betrayed someone who loved you very much and then were forgiven by that person. What were the contours of this experience? What did it feel like to be "out of covenant" with the beloved? What was it like to be reconciled? Is there anything to be learned from this experience that can help you enter into a more real and honest relationship with God?*

- *Many comfortable and successful Americans find it difficult to experience and name their creatureliness and their sinfulness. Is this true in your experience? Why is this so?*

- *If living in the truth brings life, how do we overcome our tendency to think about sin in negative, psychological categories that tear us down rather than give us life?*

- *Often we admit that we are sinners in a superficial or theoretical way simply because it is clearly outrageous and false to say that we are not. What in your own life has helped you come to terms with the truth of the depths of your sinfulness?*

- *We have noted that throughout her Prayers, Catherine*

*repeats over and over again: "I have sinned against the
Lord. Have mercy on me! Do not look at our sins, all-
powerful, compassionate, merciful God." Take some time to
pray this prayer. Resolve to drop your defenses gently,
trusting in God's love and compassion. Repeat it slowly
and reverently. Let the words sink into your being. Take
some time to reflect on what happened and to jot down the
highlights of this prayer.*

Closing Prayer

Gracious God, our sins are too heavy to carry,
    too real to hide, and too deep to undo.
Forgive what our lips tremble to name,
        what our hearts can no longer bear,
        and what has become for us a consuming fire of
        judgment.
Set us free from a past that we cannot change;
        open to us a future in which we can be changed;
        and grant us grace to grow more and more in
            your likeness and image, through Jesus
            Christ our Savior. Amen.[17]

Cancel out our sin today, then,
O true God,
and wash our soul's face
with your only-begotten Son's blood,
poured out for us,
so that dead to ourselves
and living for him
we may offer him a return for his suffering
with bright face and undivided soul.[18]

Notes

1 Edith Hamilton, *Mythology: Timeless Tales of Gods and Heroes* (New York: New American Library, 1969), p. 88.

2 Christopher Lasch, *The Culture of Narcissism: American Life in an Age of Diminishing Expectations* (New York: W. W. Norton, 1978), pp. 5, 33.

3 *Dialogue*, p. 35.

4 *Dialogue*, pp. 284-285; 311.

5 Thomas Aquinas, "Before Study," *Devoutly I Adore Thee: The Prayers and Hymns of St. Thomas Aquinas* (Manchester, N.H.: Sophia Institute Press, 1993), pp. 41-43.

6 *Letters*, p. 44.

7 *Prayers*, p. 82.

8 *Dialogue*, p. 180.

9 *Dialogue*, p. 52.

10 *Letters*, p. 127.

11 *Dialogue*, p. 29.

12 *Dialogue*, p. 186.

13 1 John 1:8.

14 John C. Haughey, *The Conspiracy of God: The Holy Spirit in Men* (Garden City, N.Y: Doubleday & Co., 1973), p. 93.

15 *Letters*, p. 80.

16 *Dialogue*, p. 53.

17 Adapted from *Book of Worship United Church of Christ*, p. 211.

18 *Prayers*, p. 65.

DAY THREE

Confronting Illusion

Coming Together in the Spirit

Joe and Sara lined up a baby-sitter for the children and headed out to a party at a friend's house. The evening progressed with the usual dose of frivolity, funny stories and teasing. Joe was having a great time. He had a few beers and got going on stories from the army and then from grad school. He was unaware of the yawns, the discreetly raised eyebrows. Nor did he notice that he wasn't giving anyone else much room to join in on the banter.

This was not the first time Sara had witnessed this behavior in Joe. But they had an open relationship and had come to rely on their care for each other and especially on honest communication.

In the car on the way home, Sara's pique got the best of her. In an exasperated tone, she confronted Joe with his negative behavior. If he monopolized the conversation at one more party, she said, he could go on his own, thank you very much! Of course, Joe's interpretation of his behavior was quite different—he saw himself as the life of the party, the *bon vivant*, the entertainer!

While few of us will admit it, many of us—at some level or other—think we are perfect. Such a view of ourselves, of course, is an illusion and can prevent us from seeing and acknowledging those particular

imperfections that are ours. Joe and Sara worked through
this difficulty as they had others in their marriage. What
they may not have been aware of is the way in which
each partner can provide a reality check for the other.
Because of their love and commitment, they were able to
help each other see the truth of who they were. This is
easier when the truth is about a virtue or gift and takes
the form of a compliment or affirmation. It is much more
challenging to deliver bad news in a way that is helpful
and productive. On some days, we will be the ones who
deliver a hard truth to another; on other days, we will be
the ones who receive it—or not. In this session, we ask
Catherine and others to teach us about the value of
naming and confronting our illusions in order to live
more fully in the truth of who we are.

Defining Our Thematic Context

On this third day of retreat, we continue to confront
the truth of the dark side of human attitudes and
behavior. Illusion can be seen from two quite different
perspectives. First, we can say that sin itself is an illusion.
This does not mean that sin is not real or truly destructive
but that the deepest truth about human beings is not that
they are sinners but that they are good because they have
been created and redeemed by God.

There is something "false" about us when we are
given to selfish and sinful behaviors. We will explore this
theme on Day Four when we reflect on this most basic
truth—that we are made in God's image and likeness.

Second, sin nurtures a desire to block out or
rationalize our sinful behaviors. We would rather live
with an illusory image of ourselves than with the truth. In
the context of our theme of truth, we can say that illusion

is a kind of lie, something false or only half-true.

Catherine was almost brutal in the way she constantly confronted herself and those around her with the falsity of their vision. She was hard on herself as she struggled throughout her life to let go of false attachments. She saw things from God's point of view, that is, from the standpoint of the gospel, and was extremely persistent in her expectations that others do the same. She invites us to explore our own story and to see how honest we are about ourselves and about the world around us.

Opening Prayer

Jesus, you opened the eyes of the blind man from Bethsaida with spittle (Mark 8: 22-26). I know I need to have my eyes opened but I am a little squeamish about your choice of healing agent. Spittle seems a bit too earthy and messy to me. What about holding me to your heart and by this touch healing me of my blindness? Or is my squeamishness a sign of my resistance? I rather like my illusions. They are comfortable and they give me status in my own eyes. But I do want to be healed of my limited and false visions. I await your healing touch.[1]

RETREAT SESSION THREE

Before we can consider sin in our life, we need to reflect on ourselves simply and realistically. Karl Rahner warns against questions like, "Am I humble or arrogant? Do I love God or not?" Rather, he says, ask, "What am I really making of my life? What am I doing?" He invites us to look at others around us, not in order to condemn them but in order to learn about ourselves. Most of us will find people who, on the whole, want to live a good life and yet we have the impression that something is terribly wrong. One is eternally self-preoccupied; another does not realize how out of touch he is with himself; and yet another may have no sense of how she overestimates or underestimates herself.[2] And yet such persons think that their moral status is perfectly in order. We need to ask, "In what ways is *that* person *me*?"

The saints have many skills when it comes to facing themselves honestly. In all religious traditions, we find customs and practices that the "holy ones" use to keep themselves on track—honest about who they are and focused on the goal. Catherine opens *The Dialogue* with these powerful words:

> A soul rises up, restless with tremendous desire for God's honor and the salvation of souls. She has for some time exercised herself in virtue and has become accustomed to dwelling in the cell of self-knowledge *in order to know better God's goodness toward her, since upon knowledge follows love. And loving, she seeks to pursue truth and clothe herself in it.*
>
> But there is no way she can savor and be enlightened by this truth as in *continual and humble prayer, grounded in the knowledge of herself and of God.*[3] (Emphasis added.)

Catherine writes not for the beginner who has not yet struggled to be virtuous or who is a stranger to introspection but for one who is "middle-aged" in the spiritual life, as it were. Catherine reminds us to get in touch with our desires for God, our desires to know the truth about ourselves and to discover God's goodness. Knowledge is a crucial first step, but it is always a step that is on its way to love. And love leads us to want to be clothed in truth. For Catherine, the way to this truth is "continual, humble prayer," the very activity in which we are presently engaged on this retreat! It may be helpful to stop for a moment to realize that this kind of prayer is not *only* something in the future. Indeed, as you pray through this retreat, you are *already* well on your way down this road of prayer.

In a much earlier chapter of the Christian story, the desert fathers and mothers had the practice of finding an "abba" or an "amma" to guide them—a wise person who was known for holiness and who was practiced in the ways of the desert. Ideally, each monk stayed with the same person for a long period of time, because it was crucial for the mentor to know the disciple well in order to offer the right counsel. Periodically the monk would go to his abba and ask for "a word." The relationship required an exacting honesty. Monks were to open their hearts totally to their mentors. This caring relationship served to keep the monks honest about themselves and gently (or in some cases, not so gently!) urged them to face their self-deceptions, to name the games they played in order to make themselves appear better than they were—to themselves or to others. The abbas also witnessed to honesty about their own lives. This honesty is visible in the following startling and puzzling sayings.

> A brother said to Abba Theodore, "Speak a word to me, for I am perishing," and sorrowfully he said to him. "I am myself in danger, so what can I say to you?"[4]

> One day Abba John was sitting down in Scetis, and the brethren came to him and asked him about their thoughts. One of the elders said, "John, you are like a courtesan who shows her beauty to increase the number of her lovers." Abba John kissed him and said, "You are quite right, Father." One of his

disciples said to him, "Do you not mind that in your heart?" But he said, "No, I am the same inside as I am outside."[5]

Abba Theodore and Abba John get our attention by their humility and their honesty about sin. The point of the first story is not that Abba Theodore didn't want to help the other monk but that he refused to be hypocritical or puffed-up about being able to help the other. He had assessed his situation honestly and was humble enough to say, "I am in danger, too."

In the second story, the elders point out something very unattractive to John about his behavior and disposition. They may be doing this because it is true, or they may be simply trying to test John. In any event, his disciples—who may still be beginners in the spiritual life—react as most of us would. They are mystified by John's gracious and accepting response and want to know why it doesn't bother him to have his faults pointed out to him. Abba John responds simply that what he does on the outside emerges from his genuine inner feelings. In both stories, the rather surprising responses are meant to get us thinking about the level of openness we have to our own sin.

One way to nurture honesty about self and others is to keep a journal. In the privacy and prayerful setting of journaling, we can take the risk of viewing our being with loving attention, and, in the Lord's presence, face the illusions within. When I think of this kind of honesty, the names of Augustine of Hippo (fourth-century North Africa) and the Quaker John Woolman (eighteenth-century North America) come immediately to mind.

Augustine never let himself off the hook about his darker side. Recall his account of stealing fruit when he was a young boy. He was with a group of boys who no doubt wanted to show off to each other by engaging in petty vandalism. Later in his life, as an adult, he reflects on his dark side, and on how God rescued him from the darkness of selfishness and sin. In his famous *Confessions*, "What fruit had I," he says, "so wretched a boy, from those deeds which I now blush to recall, especially from that theft in which I loved the theft and nothing else?... Behold the living record of my soul lies before you my God.... Who can untie this most twisted and intricate mass of knots?"[6]

One can also learn much about honest self-regard from John Woolman, the simple, unassuming Quaker, who traveled the eastern seaboard in the eighteenth century, encouraging other Quakers to abandon the practice of slavery and to wait in silence for a "way to open," revealing God's word to them. He practiced the attentive silence that gradually schooled him to hear the true word of the Spirit. He wrote in his famous journal, "This truth was early fixed in my mind, and I was taught to watch the pure opening, and to take heed lest, while I was standing to speak, my own will should get uppermost, and cause me to utter words from worldly wisdom, and depart from the channel of the true gospel ministry."[7]

Keeping a journal is only one avenue that we can take to help keep ourselves truthful. For some of us, this kind of honest self-appraisal can take place in conversation with a spiritual director who may function as our abba or amma. Ideally, spiritual direction offers an opportunity to be in a caring relationship with another "pilgrim," one whom we can trust to speak the truth of what is in our hearts and minds. As the relationship grows in trust, we may find ourselves more willing to uncover the dark side of life, to bring the most troubling or difficult aspects of ourselves into the light of the Spirit.

For others, a good friend may be the one to provide

us with a "reality check" in a loving and encouraging manner. Much will depend on how open we are to discovering those parts of ourselves that are painful or downright embarrassing. Catherine was both friend and spiritual director to many. To the monks at the monasteries of San Girolamo and Monteoliveto Maggiore, Catherine writes about the power of the baptism of blood and fire to dispel illusion. She says, "Yet let's take heart, my brothers! Our sin, or any diabolical illusion or temptation, however repulsive, filthy, and ugly it may be, need not make us falter; for our doctor has given us a medicine for any sickness we may have. I mean the baptism of blood and of fire in which the soul cleanses and washes away every sin, consumes and burns away every diabolical temptation and illusion—for the fire is steeped in blood, so it truly does burn."[8]

Catherine was even harder on clergy who failed to live up to the virtues of their office. She echoes the scathing prophetic voice of an earlier holy woman from the Rhineland, Hildegard of Bingen, who was also called by God to correct clerical abuse in the Church. Catherine writes to a parish priest of Asciano,

> Oh dearest father, give a little thought to your perilous state! In what great danger you are, drowning in this bitter sea of deadly sin! Don't we really believe that we must eventually come to the moment of death?" ... And then that poor wretched soul—who mirrors the carnal pleasures in which he wallows like a pig in mud—changes from a person into an animal in that putrid avarice of his! Many times in his greed and avarice he sells spiritual gifts and graces. He becomes swollen with pride, and spends his whole life seeking honor. And what should be given to serve the poor he spends on banquets and a host of servants and well-fed horses.[9]

Surely, this man cannot plead ignorance of his sin after receiving this letter! What gives Catherine the power and courage to speak so frankly and so specifically to a member of the clergy?

At least two things are required. First, she has to be deeply aware of her own sin. Later in this same letter she writes, "I'll say no more, but let me tell you this much: my own sins are numberless. So I promise you that I will take both mine and yours and make of them a bundle of myrrh which I will keep in my breast with constant weeping."[10] The second requirement is love. One has to be quite certain that one's motive in pointing out the faults of another is a love that is as disinterested as we can make it. Catherine's model for the Church was the crucified savior, and she loved the Church enough to challenge those who were not living up to this standard. In another letter of chastisement to a powerful and cruel nobleman in Milan, Catherine writes, "Pardon my foolish presumption. I talk very boldly, but let my love and affection for your salvation be my excuse. Keep living in God's holy and tender love."[11]

But perhaps the family is the surest and most common setting for keeping ourselves honest. The rules of behavior and interaction in a family are usually quite different from those in most other arenas of society. It may not always be the case—some families are committed to a conspiracy of silence and illusion—but, in many situations, family members are more honest with each other because they think that they won't get thrown out, no matter what they say! Living under the same roof for long periods of time usually means that family members know each other pretty well. Disgruntled siblings are likely to be quite blunt about the failings of brothers and sisters. Spouses usually call attention to each other's faults and failings when they get in the way of the relationship—we hope this is done in an atmosphere of love and support. Younger children can be counted on the most to tell the truth about family dynamics. How many of us have had last night's family altercation broadcast to the entire neighborhood or first-grade class the next morning?

Again, Catherine provides an example. In a letter to her brother, Benincasa, Catherine chastises him for neglecting their mother, Lapa. As one reads this letter, one cannot but think that some things never change! She writes:

> I don't want you to forget about making amends for your ingratitude and inattentiveness; you owe this to your mother, to whom you are obligated by God's commandment. I've seen your inattentiveness grow so much that not only have you not given her the assistance you owe her (I might hold you excused here, since you haven't had the means)—but even if you had been able I'm not so sure you would have done so, because you've scarcely kept in touch with her! Oh ingratitude! You've thought nothing of the pains of childbirth or the milk she gave you from her breast or all her trouble over you and the others.[12]

While in the moment of confrontation such revelations can be annoying—and in this case, surely guilt-inducing!—in terms of the spiritual life, they can turn out to be precious pearls of truth. For without some honest outside assessment of our behaviors, it is just too easy to start down the path of illusion, have those illusions solidify over time, and end up not knowing ourselves. Our egos seem programmed to put the best face on everything we do, even to the point of defending hurtful, sinful behaviors. Without concrete ways to keep tabs on these dispositions and actions, we risk living a life that is not in tune with the truth of ourselves, our reality and God.

Catherine was also attuned to another kind of illusion in which we think we are not capable of living an authentic Christian life. She counsels some monks not to let their souls give in to sadness or discouragement, since this is exactly what the devil wants. The devil, she says, sends lots of annoyances and struggles in order to lead the monks into unreasonable sadness and spiritual discouragement which in turn might move them to become frustrated with themselves and abandon their spiritual practices, thinking that God is not pleased with them. She continues, "When you know you have good will...then you must let go of your discouragement and walk by the light of the grace hidden within your soul, the grace God has given you in safeguarding your good will."[13] She wants them to pray for trust in the Lord Jesus to keep them safe. The darkness and confusion of spiritual sadness is also a form of illusion we must flee with God's help.

Catherine was acutely aware of her own sinfulness. She was not only not afraid to face her dark side, she pointed to it constantly. In her *Prayers*, we read the near-refrain, "My Lord, I have sinned; have mercy on me!" Sin darkens the mind's eye, making it difficult to see the light.[14] She asks for compassion and mercy "for we are blind and have no light at all."[15] Having met the God who is Truth, Catherine notices ever more acutely in herself and others that particular form of sin that we are calling illusion. We dwell in selfishness rather than in truth.

As we walk with Catherine, we can allow her to show the way, to give us the courage to face our own falseness. With the love and support of Truth and the entire communion of saints, we, too, can face ourselves honestly, name the petty games we play, begin to remove the protective walls we set up, confront the false assessments and pride-filled *personas* we create so that we may step into the ray of light into which God beckons us.

For Reflection

- *What means are present in your life that help keep you from settling into or clinging to illusion? Are there other ways you'd like to initiate to help keep you honest?*

- *Can you identify what seem to be aspects of illusion in the life of someone you know well? Now switch to your own life. Is it easy for you to name some of the illusions to which you cling? Is it rather difficult? What would you like to see happen in this regard?*

- *Name one or two people you know who seem to have the gift of honesty, simplicity and humility about themselves. What effect do they have on others? What can they teach you?*

- *Pray that God will shine the light of truth in the inmost depths of your being, leading you to honesty, clear sight and insight about yourself and your world.*

Closing Prayer

Do not consider our sins,
because of which I know I am unworthy to pray to you.
In your most merciful compassion
take away these sins of ours today.
. . .

Purify my soul,
most high God, my love,
and listen to your servant
who is calling out to you.

. . .

Just so,
once the impulses of every fleshly affection
have been cut off by your heavenly gift—
the dew of the Holy Spirit
in which you bathed the holy apostles—
let new virtues be engrafted in them
which will offer you a sweet fragrance.[16]

Notes

[1] Adapted from Macrina Wiederkehr, *The Song of the Seed: A Monastic Way of Tending the Soul* (San Francisco: HarperSanFrancisco, 1995), p. 93.

[2] Karl Rahner, *The Practice of Faith* (New York: Crossroad Publishing Co., 1992), p. 108.

[3] *Dialogue*, p. 25.

[4] *Sayings of the Desert Fathers*, trans. Benedicta Ward (Kalamazoo, Mich.: Cistercian Publications, 1975), p. 76.

[5] *Desert Fathers*, p. 96.

[6] Augustine of Hippo, *Confessions*, Vol. II. pp. 8-10.

[7] John Woolman, *The Journal of John Woolman* (Seacaucus, N.J.: The Citadel Press, 1961), p. 12.

[8] *Letters*, p. 255.

[9] *Letters*, p. 57.

[10] *Letters*, p. 58.

[11] *Letters*, p. 72.

[12] *Letters*, p. 64.

[13] *Letters*, pp. 256-57.

[14] *Prayers*, p. 89.

[15] *Prayers*, p. 129.

[16] *Prayers*, pp. 58, 60.

DAY FOUR
We Are Made in God's Image

Coming Together in the Spirit

Years ago, when I was quite young, I met Brother David Steindl-Rast at a retreat for campus ministers. When I was first introduced to him, he put his two feet together, took my hand in his, kissed it, made a profound bow and said, "How do you do?" After I recovered—I had been ready only for the traditional handshake—I reflected on the experience. I began to wonder if Brother Steindl-Rast did not see something in me that I was not always able to see in myself—that I was made in the image and likeness of God. For that moment, I stood a little taller and walked with a little more grace.

Brother Steindl-Rast's gesture stood out because the bow is not part of our cultural landscape. By contrast, in Japan, bowing is part of everyday life, from corporate deal-making to department store greetings. And in many cultures, stage performers bow before audiences and people bow as a gesture of reverence in liturgy. I suggest that the bow can serve as a symbol—a metaphor for the way we interact with one another when we become aware of and acknowledge the truth that God has made each one of us in God's image. Christian anthropology is founded on this great and glorious truth—that our loving, creator God has chosen to model the human species after God's very own image. Too bad, as Teresa of Avila says, that we do not know who we are. But if we did, what might life be like if daily we noticed this reflection of God in ourselves and in others? No doubt, there would be a lot more bowing than there is now!

Defining Our Thematic Context

The truth of our sinfulness and of our desire to nurture illusions is only one part of who we are—as Catherine would be the first to admit. Indeed, sinfulness is the more difficult and uncomfortable dimension to face, but it becomes easier when done in the context of our call to be like God. Catherine frequently reminds us that our true nature is also this: We are made in the image and likeness of God. This is the other truth about ourselves that she puts constantly before us.

Each one of us is unique. For some of us, the hard part will be coming to terms with the truth of our sinfulness. For others, it will be just the opposite. We may be all too familiar with our sinfulness, but unable to grasp the truth of the divinity that flows from our being created in God's image and likeness. Catherine is passionately convinced of our potential to be like God. This conviction is a source of great optimism for her—in spite of obstacles.

Opening Prayer

Then God said, "Let us make humankind in our
image, according to our likeness;..."
So God created humankind in his image,
in the image of God he created them;
male and female he created them.[1]

As many of you as were baptized into Christ have
clothed yourselves with Christ. There is no longer
Jew nor Greek, there is no longer slave or free, there
is no longer male and female; for all of you are one
in Christ Jesus.[2]

O great and loving God,
Let your grace flow into every fiber of my being,
Open my eyes, in all humility and simplicity,
To see my gifts, my talents,
The radiance in me that is a reflection of you.
Permit me to notice the inner and outer beauty
    you have given me,
Allow me—
To rest in your image,
To become your image,
To soothe my weary mind,
And to put on Christ.

RETREAT SESSION FOUR

Catherine's realism about the evils of her time does
not prevent her from being hopeful. The ground of that
hope is her awareness that human beings have been made
in the image and likeness of God. On the third day of our
retreat, we faced squarely into the truth of the differences
between God and us. Recall Catherine's dramatic
juxtaposition of opposites: God is life, wisdom and light;
we are death, ignorance and darkness.[3]

But the creation and the Incarnation remedy the fruits
of sin. God speaks to Catherine about Christ the bridge
that was needed because Adam's disobedience caused the

road to be so broken up that humans could not make passage to eternity. "What is this truth? That I had created them in my image and likeness so that they might have eternal life, sharing in my being and enjoying my supreme eternal tenderness and goodness. But because of their sin they never reached this goal and never fulfilled my truth, for sin closed heaven and the door of my mercy."[4]

Self-knowledge, then, encompasses both the truth of our sinfulness and the truth of our glory. Catherine captures the complex nature of self-knowledge in the following passage from *The Dialogue*:

> As the soul comes to know herself she also knows God better, for she sees how good he has been to her. In the gentle mirror of God she sees her own dignity: that through no merit of hers but by his creation she is the image of God. And in the mirror of God's goodness she sees as well her own unworthiness, the work of her own sin. For just as you can better see the blemish on your face when you look at yourself in a mirror, so the soul who in true self-knowledge rises up with desire to look at herself in the gentle mirror of God with the eye of understanding sees all the more clearly her own defects because of the purity she sees in him.[5]

Many spiritual writers in the Middle Ages employ the image of the mirror to speak about the spiritual life. In a variation of the metaphor in which the mirror becomes the open heart of Christ, Catherine invites souls to begin the journey across the bridge between earth and heaven. God speaks: "For when the soul has climbed up on the feet of affection and looked with her mind's eye into my Son's opened heart, she begins to feel the love of her own heart in his consummate and unspeakable love."[6] For Catherine, gazing into the loving heart of Christ is a way to have our own hearts transformed from stone to flesh.

Catherine thus invites us to ask what it would be like to gaze into "the gentle mirror of God" and see there our "own dignity." The truth that we are made in God's image forms a very important part of Catherine's theology. That we are created and redeemed by God in Christ makes us good. These events, or blessings, endow the human person with what Catherine calls "dignity." In a letter to Regina della Scala, the wife of a powerful Milanese nobleman who was at odds with the pope, Catherine tries to get Regina to influence her husband to reconcile with the papacy by focusing on her dignity and on how she should act because of it. Catherine begins by noting our inability to see our goodness. She writes:

> How great, then, is our wretched blindness! We see
> that we were created in God's image and likeness
> and later formed anew in grace. Yet we are so blind
> as to abandon God's affection and love which in
> God's goodness made us so great, and give
> ourselves over to loving things apart from God![7]

Our human dignity is achieved when we center on the crucified Christ rather than on ourselves. When we become one with Christ, we fulfill the basic dignity we received at creation. However, our dignity is not our own doing but comes from God. Catherine uses a human analogy to explain how we are dignified by union with Christ. When a servant maid marries an emperor, she becomes an empress, not by her own merit but because of the dignity of the emperor.[8] Today we may want to broaden the gender assignments. Just as any person grows in dignity because of the gifts of a friend or spouse or family member, so in the realm of faith, our dignity and beauty are enhanced because of the infinite grace and beauty of God. Being God's friend, Catherine wants to say, has definite, positive effects in us. We stand a little taller because we notice the grace and glory that are ours because of God's love.

Catherine's entire outlook is trinitarian and when she sees the reflection of God in human persons, it naturally takes a trinitarian form. She follows closely in the footsteps of Augustine, linking our memory, understanding and will with the three persons in God. Catherine addresses God: "You said, 'Let us make humankind in our image and likeness." And this you did, eternal Trinity, willing that we should share all that you are, high eternal Trinity!"[9] Although we no longer understand the human faculties of memory, intellect and will as medieval people did, still there is a kind of poetic beauty in linking our human capabilities with the persons in God. At the end of *The Dialogue*, Catherine offers an unusually personal prayer reflecting these ideas:

> For by the light of understanding within your light I have tasted and seen your depth, eternal Trinity, and the beauty of your creation. Then, when I considered myself in you, I saw that I am in your image. You have gifted me with power from yourself, eternal Father, and my understanding with your wisdom—such wisdom as is proper to your only-begotten Son; and the Holy Spirit, who proceeds from you and from your Son, has given me a will, and so I am able to love.[10]

Often trinitarian theology is abstract and distant, making it difficult to connect our mundane existence with the threefold nature of God. But the mystics, who speak of the Trinity from their own, very personal encounters with God, offer more vivid and accessible ways to see ourselves mirrored in the triune God. Catherine understands her own charismatic gifts as flowing from the three divine persons—power from the Creator, wisdom from the Son, a loving will from the Spirit.

To communicate the intimacy of our connection with

the triune God, Catherine employs the metaphor of human taste—the spiritual sense analogous to our physical sense of taste. She recalls Paul's experience of being drawn up to the third heaven, "to the height of the Trinity" where he "tasted and knew" God's truth through the power of the Holy Spirit.[11] Through our "spiritual vision" we see and taste "the depths of the Trinity, wholly God, wholly human."[12] She also uses the term *abyss* when she speaks of the Trinity.[13] Catherine seems to be saying to us that experiencing ourselves as images of the triune God is such a profound mystery that we need to let ourselves go into this abyss, to allow ourselves not only to "see" but also to "taste" God. It might be an interesting exercise to imagine ourselves "tasting" the Trinity. What might we discover about this often inaccessible mystery?

While Catherine sees the human person as a reflection of the Godhead, she also emphasizes—in true Thomistic fashion—the importance of reason as well as faith. Human beings are responsible to use their God-given reason, coupled with faith, to arrive at the truth. Catherine's God speaks to her: "You know that no one can walk in the way of truth without the light of reason that you draw from me, the true Light, through the eye of your understanding. If you exercise faith by virtue with the light of reason, reason will in turn be enlightened by faith, and such faith will give you life and lead you in the way of truth."[14] Catherine emphasizes that faith and reason lead us to the truth of the transitoriness of this world. And while this remains true, Christians living six hundred years later also emphasize the importance of using our reason and intelligence to learn about and use the knowledge that is available to us today—science, literature, medicine, psychology, mathematics, physics, theology and so on. Faith is not unintelligible. It is not to be put in a cubbyhole, cordoned off from the knowledge and truth that guides us in other areas of life. Rather, this knowledge should engage our reason in critical, analytical ways, and our faith should grow and be stretched by knowledge discovered by human reason.

But we may ask, "How can I make practical this truth of being made in God's image? How do we increase our ability to see the truth of who we are in God's eyes?"

First, we can imagine the face of God in prayer, gaze into it, and allow God's love to bathe us in its light, to confer grace and dignity on our lives. A contemporary of Catherine's in England, Julian of Norwich, wrote about her encounter with the loving face of the crucified.[15] Julian had a vision of the crucified upon which she meditated for decades before writing a full account of what it meant to her. She tells us that she sees in the suffering face of Christ a God not unlike the God Catherine describes. Julian calls God "homely" and "courteous" and "full loving." To both women, the cross reveals a God who is madly in love with us, and our gazing into this face is intended to reveal something about ourselves inasmuch as we are made in this God's image and likeness.

Catherine always juxtaposes knowledge of God and self-knowledge. As we come to gaze at God's loving countenance, we discover the immense beauty in ourselves and in the people and creation around us. Gazing into God's face is one way to grow and mature throughout a lifetime. Over time, we become the image we see in God's loving face. Just as children find themselves to be lovable and loved in their parents' faces, we, too, can become who we are meant to be by knowing who God is, both in prayer and in each other.

A second, and perhaps for Catherine, more important way to discover the truth of our goodness and dignity is in the faces of those around us—in the mutual loving regard that bestows warmth, acceptance, respect and care. We can reflect on experiences when we discover our God-likeness in the face of another, when we notice the beauty in ourselves because we see it reflected in the face of another. Or we can ask about what others see in our faces. Is there room in my gaze for the "other"? Do I bestow dignity on others by the way I "face" them? Surely it is a great responsibility to be the mirror of God for others in history—to reflect the truth that they are made in God's image. But what a sacred trust—that we have the power to offer a visage of hate or one of love to family and friends, colleagues and acquaintances, even enemies.

Being made in God's image means that we are called to live in the fullness of intimacy with God. And for Catherine, this fullness is reciprocal. Yes, we are made in God's image, but when God became man in Jesus, God chose to be made in our image as well! Let's listen in on the dialogue between God and Catherine. God says:

> Think of it! I gifted you with my image and likeness. And when you lost the life of grace through sin, to restore it to you I united my nature with you, hiding it in your humanity. I had made you in my image; now I took your image by assuming a human form. So I am one thing with you—except if a soul leaves me through deadly sin. But those who love me live in me and I live in them.[16]

Catherine responds:

> O depth of love! What heart could keep from breaking at the sight of your greatness descending to the lowliness of our humanity? We are your image, and now by making yourself one with us you have become our image, veiling your eternal divinity in the wretched cloud and dung heap of Adam. And why? For love! You, God became human and we have been made divine![17]

In a single gesture of love, God built a bridge between the "all" that is God and the "nothing" that is the human race. Instead of being separated by a chasm, we have the potential of becoming one both in humanity and in divinity. Catherine obviously experienced the wondrous intimacy of this joining. God says to her, "Member for member my Son joined this divine nature with yours: my power, the wisdom of my Son, the mercy of the Holy Spirit—all of me, God, the abyss of the Trinity, laid upon and united with your human nature."[18]

The Roman Catholic and Orthodox traditions hold that the image of God imprinted in our being is so powerful and enduring that even the ravages of sin cannot destroy it. As destructive as sin is, it can never wipe out the "spark" of divinity that lies at the heart of our existence. Creation and incarnation affect our humanity and all of creation—transforming reality irrevocably into something sacred. Throughout much of the Christian tradition, many theologians held that male human beings reflected God's image more perfectly than female human beings. In this century, as we struggle to overcome gender discrimination, we look to the strong women in our tradition: women who, like Catherine, were convinced of their birthright as God's beloved creatures and who inspired others—both women and men—to embrace the truth of being made in God's image. Let all the baptized, female and male, pray with Catherine: "Why did you so dignify us? With unimaginable love you looked upon your creatures within your very self, and you fell in love with us."[19]

For Reflection

■ *What are the things that keep you from embracing the*

truth that you are really made in God's image and therefore reflect God's love and goodness to the world?

- *Name those personal qualities that you judge to be most reflective of God's image.*

- *Who are the people in your life who reflect God's image most brilliantly? Take a moment to reflect on how they do this. Hold them up in a prayer of celebration, thanksgiving and blessing.*

Closing Prayer

You were taught to put away your former way of life, your old self, corrupt and deluded by its lusts, and to be renewed in the spirit of your minds, and to clothe yourselves with the new self, created according to the likeness of God in true righteousness and holiness.

So then, putting away falsehood, let all of us speak the truth to our neighbors, for we are members of one another.[20]

O great and loving God,
Allow me to rest in your image, to become your image,
To soothe my weary mind,
And to put on Christ.
Allow me to notice your image in others,
To treat others with loving deference,
And to invite them to put on Christ.

Notes

[1] Genesis 1:26-27.
[2] Galatians 3:27-28.
[3] *Prayers*, p. 82.
[4] *Dialogue*, p. 58.
[5] *Dialogue*, p. 48.
[6] *Dialogue*, p. 64.
[7] *Letters*, p. 75.
[8] *Letters*, p. 75.
[9] *Dialogue*, p. 49.
[10] *Dialogue*, p. 365.
[11] *Dialogue*, p. 152.
[12] *Dialogue*, p. 210.
[13] *Dialogue*, p. 295.
[14] *Dialogue*, pp. 184-85.
[15] Julian of Norwich, *Showings* (New York: Paulist Press, 1978).
[16] *Dialogue*, p. 46.
[17] *Dialogue*, p. 50.
[18] *Dialogue*, p. 289.
[19] *Dialogue*, p. 49.
[20] Ephesians 4:22-25.

DAY FIVE

Discernment of Spirits

Coming Together in the Spirit

The following story is told about Abba Moses, who lived as a monk in the desert at Scetis in the fourth century.

> Once the order was given at Scetis, "Fast this week." Now it happened that some brothers came from Egypt to visit Abba Moses and he cooked something for them. Seeing some smoke, the neighbours said to the ministers, "Look, Moses has broken the commandment and has cooked something in his cell." The ministers said, "When he comes, we will speak to him ourselves." When the Saturday came, since they knew Abba Moses' remarkable way of life, the ministers said to him in front of everyone, "O Abba Moses, you did not keep the commandment of men, but it was so that you might keep the commandment of God."[1]

For us, as for Abba Moses, the ultimate foundation for making good choices is the slow, steady development of one's entire life toward the good. But even for those who are well along the road of virtue, there are times when difficult decisions must be made between a true good and an apparent good; or between two goods that are competing with each other. In the story above, the wise elders realized that Moses was following a higher law that his neighbors could not see. They were still slaves to human law, even when following that law meant breaking a higher commandment—to love and be hospitable to the neighbor.

Catherine of Siena was also faced with many life situations in which she had to struggle to discern the good. She spoke about discernment as leaving her own will behind in order to take on the will of God. Discernment, she says, is like a knife that "cuts off all selfish love to its foundation in self-will."[2] Today, in our struggle to reject dualisms, we often experience God speaking *through* our natural inclinations—even though, like Catherine, we know we have to guard against selfishness and egoism. It is no easy task to thread our way through the maze of motives and complex good and evil before us each day. And it is a task that is never over; it demands a lifelong commitment.

Defining Our Thematic Context

Catherine has led us to rekindle our affections in order to meet and fall in love with a God who showers us with goodness and blessings. She has also challenged us to take stock of the truth of ourselves—both our fragility and darkness and our strength and glory. We are always both sinners and saints, and she doesn't want us to shy away from either of these truths.

Today, we move to the second phase of our retreat in which we look at truth from several vantage points. First, we will look at the gift and skill of discernment to see what Catherine has to teach us about how to distinguish the genuine good from the spurious or the evil. The story about Abba Moses points to a truth that Catherine holds dear—that it is important to focus on the interior intention of love behind the external act.

Then we will ponder freedom as a major effect of loving and living in the truth. We will end our retreat with a reflection on the gift of wisdom, which is traditionally described as a gift of the Spirit in which truth is wedded to love.

Opening Prayer

> I did not say these things to you from the beginning, because I was with you. But now I am going to him who sent me; yet none of you asks me, "Where are you going?" But because I have said these things to you, sorrow has filled your hearts. Nevertheless I tell you the truth: it is to your advantage that I go away, the Advocate will not come to you; but if I go, I will send him to you.... I still have many things to say to you, but you cannot bear them now. When the Spirit of truth comes, he will guide you into all the truth; for he will not speak on his own, but will speak whatever he hears, and he will declare to you the things that are to come. He will glorify me, because he will take what is mine and declare it to you.... Sanctify them in the truth; your word is truth. As you have sent me into the world, so I have sent them into the world. And for their sakes I sanctify myself, so that they also may be sanctified in truth.[3]

Retreat Session Five

In *The Dialogue*, God speaks to Catherine about discernment. It is "the true knowledge a soul ought to have of herself and me, and through this knowledge she finds her roots. It is joined to charity like an engrafted shoot."[4] It would seem that we have returned to Days Three and Four of this retreat! Knowledge of God and knowledge of self return as key elements in what Catherine understands by discernment. She tells us that our ability to know good from evil is grounded in our knowledge of God and self with all that this implies. As important as methods of discernment are, Catherine wants to make sure that discernment is grounded above all in our very existence. Our ability to discern aright is linked to the lifelong process of conversion. This conversion is also linked to our being made in God's image. The more one is transformed into "another Christ" the easier it is to recognize what is true and to choose on the basis of genuine love.[5]

Catherine invites us to imagine our spiritual life as a tree. The root of the tree is the source of life for the tree and all its branches, and this root is planted in the soil of humility. Humility is the fruit of our knowing that God loves us passionately and that we are sinners. As these truths become more and more part of our being, we begin to think as God does, to choose as God would, to think of others rather than of ourselves. The ability to discern means that we are able to see and give proper due to God, to ourselves, to others.

True discernment is the ability to see the world more and more as God sees it—with the eyes of love. As we grow in our ability to look upon the world with a loving, contemplative gaze, the more we are likely to act toward others as we would like and as they deserve as beloved creatures of God. The humility needed for discernment is also connected to charity. Catherine tells us that "humility is the governess and wet nurse of the charity into which this branch of discernment is engrafted."[6] We make bad decisions when pride gets a foothold in us. We make good choices in life, above all, because we love.

In an echo of the story of Moses, Catherine underlines the importance of interior disposition over external action. Everything we do should be done in the light of genuine self-knowledge and knowledge of God's goodness. For example, fasting without discernment, she says, is like focusing on the fast itself or upon feelings of arrogance because one is able to fast. The true motive and goal of fasting—love of God—recedes from view. We can apply this principle to many of the situations we face in our lives. We may rationalize poor discernment and poor choices because they are easier or safer, or because they don't rock the boat, or because they don't disturb our vested interests. Fear or indifference can block our ability to discern the truly good from the spurious.

Discernment that involves bypassing law or custom must be undertaken with great care. We need the counsel of those who are knowledgeable and wise. We need to enter into deep prayer in which we open ourselves as fully and honestly as possible to the light of the Holy Spirit. Also required is a profound trust that God will guide us and all those involved in making such an important decision. Catherine also specifies three priorities in discernment. First, all our powers should be directed toward serving God courageously and conscientiously. Second, we must love our neighbors and be willing to bear any pain for their salvation. Third, we must put material possessions at the service of the neighbor's physical needs.[7]

Sin prevents us from discerning rightly. It causes us to make false judgments because we can no longer see rightly. In the context of truth, sin refers to ignorance, to falseness, to lies. In sin, things get turned upside down. What is truly good strikes us as a bad idea. What is truly sin becomes appealing. Sinners, says Catherine, are constantly scandalized by God's ways. Jesus had such detractors around him, criticizing him for curing on the Sabbath or for having compassion on society's outcasts. Catherine speaks about sin in terms of rottenness and losing one's taste. "Because they are rotten to the core and have spoiled their sense of taste, good things seem evil to them and evil (that is, disordered living) seems good."[8]

For Catherine, the devil is ever vigilant, luring us to this "upside down world." The devil blinds us with pleasure and honors in this world. He catches us "with the hook of pleasure under the guise of good," knowing that we will be drawn to evil only under the appearance of some pseudo-good.[9] Without the gift and skills of discernment, we are unable to notice the difference. Our self-interest blinds us to the true good. Catherine speaks of two kinds of delusion that prevent true discernment. The first is when we define spiritual consolation in our own way. Many of us demand that we "feel good" in an egotistic way when we follow God's way. Then when this good feeling disappears we are tempted to go back to our old ways rather than open ourselves to the truth of Christ crucified.

The second kind of delusion seeks spiritual peace and quiet over the needs of our neighbors.[10] We can succumb to a kind of "neatness" and satisfaction in our spiritual lives that comes from going to church, praying regularly, contributing to charity—and feeling pretty good about ourselves. In this state, we may not feel the need to reach out to the messy situations of life that cry out for our attention and care. Catherine writes about the person who gets spiritually arrested, stopping at the pleasure of visions or consolations. She "finds so much pleasure in the consolation that her gladness over receiving what she loves does not let her see or care about" discernment.[11]

The authentic sign of truth, says Catherine, is the presence of gladness and hunger for virtue, especially the virtues of true humility and blazing charity.[12] We have to be able to tell when the gladness of consolation is genuine. We can judge wrongly that the consolation is a sign that everything is in order. Catherine's own life exemplifies this second delusion, when she was directed away from the controlled solitude of the "cell" in her home to the turmoil of caring for the poor and sick and responding to her call to a more public mission in Church and society. It is clear that this mission brought her grief beyond her imagining. Only her loving will to follow God's call, coupled with her ability to discern the truly good thing to do, allowed her to cope with all the suffering that came in its wake.

For Catherine, discernment is directly related to knowledge and truth. She employs her now familiar image of light to describe it. She writes:

> Discernment is that light which dissolves all darkness, dissipates ignorance, and seasons every virtue and virtuous deed. It has a prudence that cannot be deceived, a strength that is invincible, a constancy right up to the end, reaching as it does from heaven to earth, that is, from the knowledge of me to the knowledge of oneself, from love of me to love of one's neighbors.[13]

This light is foundational to other aspects of the spiritual life. God says to Catherine, "those who do not recognize good and the cause of good, that is, virtue, can neither love nor desire me, Goodness itself, or the virtue I have given you as a means and instrument for grace from me, the true God."[14] Catherine invites us to step back and think about how skilled we are at discerning the true good from the false or pseudo-good. This is not always easy. But we do have some signs by which we know we are recognizing the true good, that is, the virtues and the fruits and gifts of the Holy Spirit. Are we growing in our ability to love, to be at peace, to be patient, long-suffering, magnanimous?

Many people who knew Catherine looked to her to help them discern God's presence and will in their lives. She could be quite directive in helping her disciples discern what to do. But she also encouraged them to be attentive to God's will themselves in order to arrive at the best decision. Catherine writes to Frate Tommaso della Fonte:

> It seems to me you are planning to go somewhere else. [He had written about a visit to the body of Saint Agnes, possibly a reference to a pilgrimage to the monastery at Montepulciano where Agnes' body was preserved.] I didn't think you ought to do that now, but let it be the way God and you want it. May God give you grace to choose the best course in this, and make all you do serve his honor and the good of your soul.[15]

Discernment involves having a clear view on the situation in light of our faith and of the truth of who God is and what God wants of us.[16] We may think that this is easy for the saints, and in a sense, it is, because they love much. But the saints are rarely spared the struggles and agonies the discernment process can entail. Catherine certainly fits this description. In his *Life of Catherine of Siena*, Raymond of Capua details her anguish. Catherine worried about engaging in public actions, traveling, spending time in the company of men—all forbidden to women by medieval Italian society. And yet she braved much criticism in order to carry out what she saw as the will of God for her. One can almost hear the cattiness and outrage: "Why is that one gadding about so much? She's a woman. Why doesn't she stay in her cell, if it's God she wants to serve?"[17] And on her deathbed, Catherine was plagued with doubts about whether her life had indeed been grounded in God's will or in her own. And, sometimes, good discernment entails being willing to be foolish in the eyes of the world, embracing instead a kind of divine foolishness that makes sense only in the context of a faithful commitment to gospel living.

Catherine can keep us company when we have difficult, even agonizing, decisions to make about important things for ourselves, our families and our world. In responding with all her heart to what she heard God calling her to do, she found herself in many ambiguous situations in which she took on unconventional religious roles and in which the vested interests of many different parties clamored for her attention. Her life is a life filled with moments of discernment, in which she had to sort out good and evil with prayer and perseverance. Her love and commitment to the truth serve as a model for anyone who strives to be a faithful Christian in our morally amorphous and complex world.

For Reflection

- Close your eyes and imagine yourself as a tree with your roots reaching down into the moist earth for nurture and growth. Imagine that your root system reaches out into the soil of humility. How can growth in the virtue of humility enhance your ability to discern good and evil spirits?

- Is there an area in your life that calls for discernment? Invite Catherine to walk with you as you hold this area of your life before the loving gaze of God. Reflect prayerfully on the various options and invite the Spirit to enlighten *you with the truth that will lead to goodness for you and for others.*

■ *Have there been times in your life when you discerned that the right thing to do meant stepping out of accepted roles, taking a risk, standing up for someone or something when it wasn't popular to do so? What did you choose to do and why? Reflect on this experience in light of Catherine's courage to follow the good, even when it brought on suffering and ridicule.*

Closing Prayer

Live by the Spirit, I say, and do not gratify the desires of the flesh. For what the flesh desires is opposed to the Spirit, and what the Spirit desires is opposed to the flesh; for these are opposed to each other, to prevent you from doing what you want. But if you are led by the Spirit, you are not subject to the law. Now the works of the flesh are obvious: fornication, impurity, licentiousness, idolatry, sorcery, enmities, strife, jealousy, anger, quarrels, dissensions, factions, envy, drunkenness, carousing, and things like that....By contrast, the fruit of the Spirit is love, joy, peace, patience, kindness, generosity, faithfulness, gentleness, self-control.[18]

Notes

[1] *The Sayings of the Desert Fathers*, p. 139.

[2] *Dialogue*, p. 43.

[3] John 16: 4b-7; 12-14; 17:17-19.

[4] *Dialogue*, p. 40.

[5] See Diana L. Villegas, "Discernment in Catherine of Siena," *Theological Studies* 58 (1997), p. 24, and "Spiritual Discernment in *The Dialogue* of Saint Catherine of Siena," *Horizons* 9/1 (1982), pp. 47-59.

[6] *Dialogue*, p. 40.

[7] *Dialogue*, p. 44.

[8] *Dialogue*, pp. 76, 175.

[9] *Dialogue*, p. 89.

[10] *Dialogue*, pp. 129-30.

[11] *Dialogue*, p. 199.

[12] *Dialogue*, p. 198.

[13] *Dialogue*, p. 44-45.

[14] *Dialogue*, p. 186.

[15] *Letters*, p. 45.

[16] *Dialogue*, pp. 92, 185.

[17] Raymond of Capua, pp. 116-117, 339.

[18] Galatians 5:16-21a, 22-23.

Day Six

'The Truth Will Make You Free' (JOHN 8:32)

Coming Together in the Spirit

There is a Hindu story that goes like this:

In India hunters had a proven way of catching
monkeys. A half coconut would be hollowed out
and a hole made that was only large enough to let a
monkey's open hand pass through. The coconut was
then pinned to the ground and tempting food placed
beneath. A monkey would approach, intent on
getting hold of the food beneath the coconut, but
alas as soon as it grasped the food in its fist it found
itself unable to pull its hand and the food free of the
coconut. Imprisoned it would stay, caught by its
own unwillingness to open its fist.[1]

We are often unaware of our closed and grasping fists.
The commercial aspects of our culture are so pervasive
we may not even realize that our clinging leads us out of
true freedom into confinement. When false values invade
our lives, we can become enslaved to them—no longer
enjoying the freedom of the children of God.

Freedom from care was also a value among the desert
fathers and mothers. In this literature, there are several
stories about robberies that invite us to focus on our
unfreedoms.

> The same old man [Euprepius] helped some thieves
> when they were stealing. When they had taken
> away what was inside his cell, Abba Euprepius saw
> that they had left his stick and he was sorry. So he
> took it and ran after them to give it to them. But the
> thieves did not want to take it, fearing that
> something would happen to them if they did. So he
> asked someone he met who was going the same way
> to give the stick to them.[2]

This parable-like story is outrageous to our sensibilities.
While our energy is usually focused on protecting our
possessions, Euprepius not only didn't have many things,
but gloried in having less and in making sure that others
had what they wanted, even though what they wanted
belonged to him! Catherine, too, was penetrating in her
perceptions about those things that keep us in slavery,
counseling others to live in freedom. John's Gospel
reminds us that if we keep God's word we will know the
truth that will make us free.[3] Ultimately, our freedom
rests in the truth that Jesus came to set us free—free from
sin and free for the service of others.

Defining Our Thematic Context

Throughout this retreat, we have been assembling
elements of truth that, in the end, can make us free. One
of the first steps toward freedom is an honest assessment
of our weaknesses and egoisms. This admission frees us
from worry about preserving our "flawless" self-image
before others which drains us of energy and creativity.

Catherine wants us to experience both our total
dependence on God—necessary because we are nothing—
and total trust in God's providence, which allows us to
live in freedom. In *The Dialogue* God says, "I always

provide, and I want you to know that what I have given humankind is supreme providence."[4] God created us in God's image and likeness, so that we might understand and enjoy God and rejoice in God's goodness. God says, "My providence will never fail those who want to receive it."[5] We wonder whether relying on the Lord was easier or harder in the fourteenth century than it is now. Certainly the fragility of life was present then, albeit in ways that were different from today. Perhaps medieval people were not so cynical as we seem to be. But casting one's care upon the Lord—as Psalm 54 tells us—is surely no easier now than it was then, and yet it is essential to a life of freedom. Today we pray for growth in confidence in the sustaining, loving, providential care of God, so that we might indeed live in the freedom of God's children.

Opening Prayer

Then Jesus said to the Jews who had believed in him, "If you continue in my word, you are truly my disciples; and you will know the truth, and the truth will make you free." They answered him, "We are descendants of Abraham and have never been slaves to anyone. What do you mean by saying, 'You will be made free'?"

Jesus answered them, "Very truly, I tell you, everyone who commits sin is a slave to sin. The slave does not have a permanent place in the household; the son has a place there forever. So if the Son makes you free, you will be free indeed."[6]

Retreat Session Six

Catherine emphasizes freedom in all her writings. It is a very important element in her understanding of the spiritual life. She describes the human person as having three gates—memory, understanding and will. In order to lead us toward a more perfect love, according to Catherine, God allows us to be tempted in the first two areas, but never in the third. No enemies can open up the gate of the will, which is the main gate guarding the city of the soul. The guard at this gate always remains free to say yes or no as he pleases. But if he says yes to sin, then the enemy of selfish love and all the other enemies that accompany it follow after and come into the soul.[7]

Catherine's idea of the spiritual life is one of adult maturity and responsibility. When the soul is old enough to discern good from evil she can choose one or the other in freedom as it pleases her. Catherine writes:

> But such is the freedom of your humanity, and so strong have you been made by the power of this glorious blood, that neither the devil nor any creature can force you to the least sin unless you want it. You were freed from slavery so that you might be in control of your own powers and reach the end you were created for. How wretched you would be, then, to wallow in the mud like an animal, ignoring the great gift I had given you![8]

Catherine would *not* be sympathetic to the excuse, "The devil made me do it!"

Catherine appealed to human freedom in many of the settings of her life. In one of these roles, she functioned as a mediator between various warring parties. One such quarrel was between the pope and a powerful political figure in Milan, Bernabo Visconti. In a letter to Bernabo in which she tries to get him to submit to the pope's

demands, Catherine places the spotlight on freedom.
Catherine wants Bernabo to focus not on the lordship of
earthly cities, but on the lordship of his own soul. She
says of the city of the soul, "So strong is this city and such
a perfect realm that neither the devil nor anyone else can
seize it unless we ourselves consent. It is never lost except
through deadly sin.... No one can force us to commit the
slightest sin, because God has put *yes* and *no* into the
strongest thing there is, into our will."[9] The saints, she
continues, say that God's servants are the ones who are
free sovereigns; they have won the victory. This victory is
possible because Christ, "the spotless Lamb, gave himself
up to the shameful death of the most holy cross in order
to restore our liberty and make us free."[10] Our enemies
are not other people, but the world, the flesh and the
devil. She encourages Bernabo to strike "these enemies
down with the hand of free choice. Do not hesitate, for
this hand is strong, this sword powerful...and no one can
wrest it from you."[11] Catherine's personality is described
by some as "willful." This may have been so—certainly
she was not shy about asserting what she thought was
best. But clearly, she believed that, in Christ, she and
others had great willpower to say no to sin and to choose
the good.

When we experience the freedom of the daughters
and sons of God, we are moved to speak and act out of
that freedom. But first, we might ask "freedom from
what?" and "freedom for what?" In terms of our theme of
truth, we can begin by saying that God's freedom is
freedom from illusions and the fears that accompany
them. Being in a love relationship with God and living in
the truth brings a kind of quiet confidence because we are
not living out of a false or inflated ego. We are less
worried about building up a certain "image" of ourselves
and then protecting that image at all costs. When we no

longer expend a lot of energy preserving ourselves or hanging on to things or accomplishments, we are more likely to live out of a kind of self-forgetfulness or abandon that confounds more calculating behaviors.

The freedom of God is *for* love, for concern for the other, especially those who are most fragile, neglected or oppressed. When we are in love, we take offenses committed against those we love very personally, and we are motivated to speak and act on their behalf. This behavior, however, inevitably creates difficulties. Genuine love often leads to the freedom to challenge the status quo, to offer a prophetic word, to condemn injustice. And so the virtue of courage is an important corollary to living in the freedom of the truth. God says to Catherine, "Thus, as soon as you and my other servants come in this way to know my truth you will for the glory and praise of my name, have to endure great trials, insults, and reproaches in word and deed, even to the point of death."[12]

On the second day of our retreat, we noted how Catherine held others accountable for their choices of good or evil. In *The Dialogue*, God says of those who are ungrateful that "they have, with the hand of free choice, encrusted their hearts in a diamond rock that can never be shattered except by blood." Still, in spite of their hardness, God wants them, while they still have time and freedom, to choose to seek the blood of Christ and pour his blood over the hardness of their hearts.[13] Free will is a gift of God, created in us as part of our nature. The freedom of the children of God is the fruit of being in love with God.

In our culture, many people associate freedom with the ability to "do what I want," to make superficial choices about where to live or what job to choose. Catherine's idea of freedom is more in line with that of Paul, who says to the Galatians, "For freedom Christ has set us free. Stand firm, therefore, and do not submit again to a yoke of slavery.... For you were called to freedom, brothers and sisters; only do not use your freedom as an opportunity for self-indulgence, but through love become slaves to one another."[14] One goal of Christian freedom is to love our neighbor as ourselves.

Our faith allows us a glimpse into the truth of reality—that we are loved and saved by a kind, honest and trustworthy God. To the extent that we stray from this truth, to the extent that our vision grows cloudy or dim, to that extent do we jeopardize our freedom. Unfreedom assumes many forms of fear, anxiety and paralysis. We are prone to obsessive anxiety about the future. We relive the struggles of yesterday and preview those of tomorrow. We may have undue remorse about past mistakes and wrong turns. We are anxious about preserving a certain image of ourselves and about becoming vulnerable and open to others. We worry about losing our possessions, our status, our security.

Our unfreedoms prevent us from being free to love others; from enjoying the love and beauty around us as children enjoy their play in innocent and unaffected simplicity. Of course, we need to discern between the legitimate concerns we take on as responsible members of the human race and those self-centered cares that encroach on our freedom. As we have seen, Catherine's teaching on discernment can serve us well as we strive both to use our God-given freedom wisely and to learn from the "lilies of the field."

Many years ago, in a course on the Psalms, the professor was trying to communicate to us the freedom grounding the psalms of praise. To make his point, he characterized human beings as either "memo-writers" or "hymn-singers." "Memo-writers" are people whose anxieties and fears lead them to try to control and

manipulate their environment and the people around
them. Rather than face-to-face conversation and
communication, they write "memos" and stick them in
other peoples' mailboxes. In contrast, "hymn-singers" are
those who are able to abandon themselves to providence,
to sing and dance and play cymbals—even in the midst of
extreme suffering. He used the example of African-
American slaves dancing and singing "Amazing Grace"
during their clandestine worship in the open fields of
nature. "Memo-writers" are those who always think that
life "owes" them something, and they become bitter when
life inevitably lets them down. On the other hand,
"hymn-singers" experience life as gift. They are the true
contemplatives for whom gratitude is a basic disposition
out of which they live their lives each day. These images
can help us locate the traces of "memo-writing" and
"hymn-singing" in ourselves. The former is set in the
context of freedom but is really a sign of enslavement.
The latter is set in the context of slavery, but in reality
points to genuine freedom.

Catherine's life is a witness to her trust in God's
providence. She opened herself to the freedom that
allowed her both to "let go" and to "lead" courageously
in arenas normally forbidden to women. She lived her life
with a kind of abandon that is the hallmark of a free child
of God. By throwing herself in trust on God's care and
mercy, she overcame her fears, allowing an ever more
spacious wisdom to emerge. She held herself accountable
to use her God-given freedom to choose the good and
turn her back on temptation and evil inclinations.

Freedom is not primarily an individual experience
but is deeply embedded in community relationships.
Catherine invited her friends to be free. It is clear from
her writings that they were very important to her, and by
offering them up to the Lord, she freed them to do the

Lord's work more effectively. She chastised them when
worrying about themselves led them away from God's
mission. Catherine's concern for her friends, her constant
prayer for them and the way she held them up before
God allowed them to be free *from* worry about themselves
and *for* the work God had entrusted to them. Her letters
are full of examples of such encouragement and support.
Catherine almost always began her letters as she did this
one to Frate Bartolomeo Dominici: "I, Caterina, servant
and slave of God's servants, am writing to encourage you
in the precious blood of God's Son. I long to see you so
engulfed and set on fire in Christ Jesus that you will be
completely lost to yourself."[15] And in a letter to an Abbess
and Sister of Santa Marta in Siena she writes, "I, Caterina,
a useless servant of Jesus Christ, and yours too, want to
do for you a servant's work of delivering and fetching. So
I want to carry you constantly into the presence of the
most gentle Savior, and once I have brought you there, we
shall ask his unutterable charity for grace to come back
down, doing the other job servants do."[16]

Every person has the responsibility to exercise her or
his priesthood, that is, to offer up to the Lord as an
oblation other people, all species and the earth itself.
When we focus our energies on holding others up before
God, they become free—no longer having to do this for
themselves. If I know that those around me are holding
me up, offering me daily before the Lord, surely I can live
with more abandon and self-forgetfulness. This is a grave
and glorious responsibility and sacred opportunity that
we have toward one another. In a very real way, each
person's freedom can be enhanced when others raise up
their very being and existence to God.

From the beginning, Catherine has plotted a course
leading to freedom. She introduced us to the God who is
"Gentle Truth" and through knowledge of this God and

of self, she invites us to live in the truth of existence, learn to see the world with God's loving gaze, trust in God's providence, and thus be able to choose to love—God, ourselves, others and our world—in confidence and freedom. As we will see, to let go and to live in freedom allows us to live wisely as well. Catherine had great confidence in our ability to make good use of the gift of freedom. She realized that traveling light makes us more open to the present moment and its graces. She holds us accountable to choose the good, to use our freedom wisely.

For Reflection

- *It is important for each of us to test whether the gospel saying that the "truth shall make you free" really means something in our lives. Can you identify an experience in your life in which you got derailed from the truth? Did you experience a kind of unfreedom? What did it feel like? What were its consequences? What did you do about it?*

- *Often we are unfree because we are afraid. Can you identify a major fear in your life that makes you timid and hesitant to live in the freedom of the children of God?*

- *When have you felt most free? What images or metaphors come to mind? Reflect on how you might link this experience with your own growth in the Spirit, with your willingness to live in the truth.*

- *We have an enormous influence on those around us. How does your freedom or unfreedom affect your family, colleagues at work, neighbors, people who suffer across the globe?*

Closing Prayer

God, Eternal Mystery of our Being, You have set us free because Your own infinity has become the limitless horizon of our life. You gathered us into safety by making everything but Your own infinitude provisional for us. You have made us present to Yourself by perpetually destroying all idols in us and around us. We want to worship them but they turn us to stone. It is because You alone are our infinite goal that we have an immense movement of hope ahead of us. If we truly and totally believed in You as the One Who gave Himself to us, we would be truly free. You promised us this victory since Jesus of Nazareth gained it in His death, for Himself and His brothers and sisters, by once more finding You as His Father even in the death of abandonment. In Him, Jesus of Nazareth, the Crucified and Risen One, we know for sure that neither ideas nor powers and dominions, neither the burden of tradition nor the utopian ideas of our futures, neither the gods of reason nor the gods of our own depths, nor really anything in or around us, can separate us from *that* love in which the unspeakable God...in all-embracing freedom has given [God]self to us in Christ Jesus, our Lord. Amen. [17]

Notes

[1] *Stories of the Spirit, Stories of the Heart: Parables of the Spiritual Path from Around the World*, eds. Christina Feldman and Jack Kornfield (San Francisco: HarperSanFrancisco, 1991), p. 345.

[2] *The Sayings of the Desert Fathers*, p. 62.

[3] John 8:31-32.

[4] *Dialogue*, p. 277.

[5] *Dialogue*, p. 280

[6] John 8: 31-36.

[7] *Dialogue*, p. 299.

[8] *Dialogue*, p. 53.

[9] *Letters*, p. 68.

[10] *Letters*, p. 69.

[11] *Letters*, p. 69.

[12] *Dialogue*, p. 30.

[13] *Dialogue*, pp. 31-32.

[14] Galatians 5:1, 13

[15] *Letters*, p. 47.

[16] *Letters*, p. 38.

[17] Karl Rahner, *Prayers for a Lifetime* (New York: Crossroad Publishing Co., 1985), p. 88.

DAY SEVEN
'Come, O Wisdom!'

Coming Together in the Spirit

When a group of women met to discuss the scriptural books of wisdom, one of the women told this Jewish story:

> A great rabbi spent years in solitude meditating on the mystery of the divine in all things. When he finally returned to live among men and women his eyes shone with the beauty of what he discovered. Many seekers came to him to ask for his truth, yet he was always reluctant to answer them, to put it into words. Pressed for years he finally relented and with eloquent words gave a feeble approximation of what he had discovered.
>
> The seekers took these words with them everywhere. They spoke them, wrote them, created sacred texts about them, and religious societies were formed of those who repeated them, until no one remembered that the words were really about an experience. As his words spread, the rabbi became disheartened. "I had hoped to help but perhaps I should not have spoken at all."[1]

Talk about wisdom is necessary and important, but the rabbi reminds us to keep our focus on the experience, to seek anew the insight of wisdom and the gift of wisdom in each generation.

This particular evening, the women planned to celebrate in ritual their common labor and their ties to each other. The ritual was simple and moving. After several short readings from the wisdom books, they were asked to name the wisdom figures in their lives—persons who embodied the gift of wisdom for them and for the world in a special way. The women spoke of mothers and grandmothers; mentors and spouses; children and friends. There were stories of selfless dedication, of challenge, of feeling loved and cared for, of insight and blessing, of joy and dancing. After a silence, each woman anointed the forehead of the woman next to her with fragrant oil. Personal prayers were offered—gratitude for gifts given and shared; celebration of generous love; blessings for insight; petitions that they continue to open themselves to the gift of wisdom and thus be able to pass it on to future generations.

Catherine of Siena's circle of close friends depended on her for wisdom and she honored that expectation whenever she could. She attended with great care to their individual personalities, their needs and faults, their gifts. As she died, she called each one to her and commissioned them to carry out their particular mission as she envisioned it. She was wise because she responded to Eternal Truth and Love with every fiber of her being—a response that was carried out primarily toward her neighbors. She wedded truth to love in her own unique way, and she challenges us to do the same.

Defining Our Thematic Context

We arrive at our final way-station on this retreat walk with Catherine of Siena. Step by step we have listened to her wisdom, taking up her invitation to see the many facets of truth that refract in our lives like the facets of a diamond. We turn now, in true Catherinian fashion, to that truth and knowledge that, when wedded to love, we call wisdom—the first-named of the seven gifts of the Holy Spirit. With Thomas Aquinas, Catherine held that knowledge has a certain primacy since we cannot love what we do not know. But love is the goal and the crown—both of God's gestures toward us and of our gestures toward God, self and especially others. Catherine's God says, "I want you to be a lover of all things, because they are all good, perfect, and worthy of love"[2]

Opening Prayer

Does not wisdom call,
and does not understanding raise her voice?
. . .

at the entrance of the portals she cries out:
"To you, O people, I call,
. . .

O simple ones, learn prudence;
acquire intelligence, you who lack it.
Hear, for I will speak noble things,
and from my lips will come what is right;
for my mouth will utter truth;
. . .

All the words of my mouth are righteous;
there is nothing twisted or crooked in them.
. . .

Take my instruction instead of silver,
and knowledge rather than choice gold;
for wisdom is better than jewels,

and all that you may desire cannot compare with her."

. . .

I love those who love me,
and those who seek me diligently find me.[3]

Retreat Session Seven

People in Catherine's time were struck by her wisdom. She attracted a loyal band of followers who saw and were drawn to her wisdom. In the First Prologue to her *Life*, Raymond of Capua frequently calls attention to Catherine's wisdom. Catherine "unlocked the secrets of the wisdom of God for many souls"; Eternal Wisdom chose "saintly young women" so that foolish men might learn where to find true wisdom and virtue, light and peace. And in his enthusiasm for her sanctity, he says that Catherine "penetrated into the abyss of divine wisdom as deeply as any soul who is still a pilgrim here below may do," opening and unfolding its mysteries to the rest of us.[4] And when Catherine was called to extend her mission beyond the walls of Siena, she received assurances from God. Raymond of Capua records God's message to her:

> The salvation of many souls requires that you not inhabit your cell anymore. You must leave even your own city for the salvation of souls. I will always be with you, and I will lead you forth and I will bring you back. You will carry the honor of My name and My spiritual warnings to the small and the great, as much to lay people as to clerics and religious. And I will give you a mouth and a wisdom that no one will be able to resist.[5]

And finally, in 1970, when Catherine was declared a
Doctor of the Church, Pope Paul VI commented on her
wisdom. "What strikes us most about the Saint is her
infused wisdom. That is to say, lucid, profound and
inebriating absorption of the divine truths and the
mysteries of the faith contained in the Holy Books of the
Old and New Testaments...due to a charism of wisdom
from the Holy Spirit."[6]

As we noted on our first day of retreat, the term *truth*
is most often associated with knowledge of the mind.
This kind of knowledge is the fruit of study, of attentive
and prolonged reflection or of skills mastered. It produces
a certain kind of excellence that is sorely needed in our
world. But for some people, in certain arenas of their
lives, this knowledge is enhanced with the gift of love.
Love affects one's motivation and can affect one's
learning. Some scientists report that they gain deeper
insight into the things they study when they are able to
identify with them, or even "fall in love" with them! The
quest to discover cures for disease can be positively
affected when the researcher is in love with, and full of
compassion for, those who suffer from the disease. The
moral person who is in love will discover a hundred
solutions to a problem of injustice, while the one who just
keeps the law will find but a few. When knowledge is
linked to love our creativity is set flowing.

When we turn to the gospel, we can distinguish
between having a certain intellectual expertise and being
in love with the word of God. All of us should have some
of both. Knowing about the background and formation of
the Bible should not be left to the biblical scholars, nor
does any one group have a corner on the Spirit's gift of
wisdom. The person who is genuinely in love with God
will have insight into the truth of the gospel at a level
quite different from that of one who regards the gospel

only as an object of study.

In a famous passage in *The Dialogue*, Catherine speaks of how the gift of charity, found in the blood of Christ, enlightens the minds of both the famous Doctors of the Church and of the ordinary people to understand the Scriptures. The fire of charity comes forth and "carries off their heart and spirit." Then their mind's eye rises up and gazes into the Godhead, and love follows understanding to be nourished there and brought into union. This is a vision that through infused grace God gives to the soul who loves and serves God in truth.[7] Through love, God sends lamps to enlighten blind and dense understanding to enable us to know the truth in the midst of darkness.

God speaks, "So what had seemed darksome before now appears most perfectly lightsome to every sort of person—to the dense as to the discerning. All receive according to their capacity and according to their readiness to know me, for I do not spurn their dispositions."[8] Wisdom is available to everyone, because everyone has the freedom to choose love. Catherine writes of the importance of love to her friend and spiritual director, Tommaso della Fonte, *"Love, sweet love! Open, open up our memory for us, so that we may receive, hold fast, and understand God's great goodness!* For as we understand, so we love, and when we love, we find ourselves united with and transformed in love, in this mother charity, having passed through and yet ever passing through the gate that is Christ crucified."[9]

Catherine also notes the effect that love has on the practice of the virtues. We are all familiar with the famous passage in Paul's first letter to the Corinthians in which he says, "If I speak in the tongues of mortals and of angels...understand all...knowledge...give away all my possessions...but do not have love, I gain nothing."[10] Catherine may have had Paul in mind when she writes that charity gives life to all the virtues, indeed they cannot exist without it. God says, "In other words, virtue is attained only through love of me."[11] The wedding of knowledge and love can produce the fruits of wisdom in our activity as well as in our knowledge.

Our retreat director links wisdom with all three persons of the Trinity. It is the Father's wisdom that provided for creation and providential care of the world.[12] Most often, Catherine links wisdom with Christ.[13] And it is the Holy Spirit who comes to bring us the fruits of Christ's wisdom.[14] The Holy Spirit was sent to ensure that the legacy of wisdom would be carried down the generations. In *The Dialogue* God says, "He [the Holy Spirit] came with my power and my Son's wisdom and his own mercy...to make even more firm the road my Truth had left in the world through his teaching."[15]

Catherine speaks of the way God shares God's wisdom with the soul. "In that same charity I shared with her the wisdom of my Son, and in that wisdom she saw and came to know, with her mind's eye, my truth and the delusions of spiritual sensuality, that is, the imperfect love of one's own consolation."[16] God says to Catherine, "And I am very displeased with those who do not knock in truth at the door of Wisdom, my only-begotten Son, by following his teaching."[17]

Our mentor teaches us that not only must we pray for the gift of wisdom, but that we must share it with others in and through the power of the Holy Spirit. "To the Holy Spirit is appropriated fire, and to the Son, wisdom. And in that wisdom my ministers receive a gracious light for administering this light with lightsome gratitude for the blessing they received from me the eternal Father when they followed the teaching of this Wisdom, my only-begotten Son."[18] Catherine's own willingness to put her wisdom at the disposal of the community reminds us of

Paul's first letter to the Corinthians. He writes, "But we speak God's wisdom, secret and hidden, which...God has revealed to us through the Spirit; for the Spirit searches everything, even the depths of God.... [N]o one comprehends what is truly God's except the Spirit of God."[19]

Near the end of his life, the German theologian, Karl Rahner, wrote a book entitled *Prayers for a Lifetime.* In the prayer, "God of Knowledge," he says that we can approach the true heart of reality only through knowledge joined to its full flower, love. Only "knowledge gained through experience, the fruit of living and suffering, fills the heart with the wisdom of love."[20] He calls wisdom "the golden harvest" of what we have lived and suffered. Wisdom comes from having met life and the Lord in joy and suffering. Rahner prays, "Your Word and Your Wisdom are in me, not because I comprehend you with my understanding, but because I have been recognized by You as Your child and friend."[21]

In the end, wisdom is the fruit of a love affair with God. It is relational. Catherine, too, paid attention to the God of her life. She met God in her living, her loving, her praying, her suffering. Her confidence and her appeal to others were no doubt based on this "grassroots" experience, that when trusted, blossoms into wisdom. We tend to link wisdom with long experience, and many reflective and loving people do shine with wisdom as they age gracefully. But we all know about the wisdom of children and that of the individual who is open to this gift at any stage in life. Wisdom is not something I can call up or demand in prayer. But we are told to pray for what we need, and so it is eminently appropriate to pray for this special gift of the Holy Spirit.

While the gift of wisdom may not always develop quickly or easily in us, we can recognize it when we see it in others or when we benefit from it. At root, the wise person is imbued with a love of others, of the world, of God. Catherine's writings are centered on God, but as she often repeats, "every good and every evil is done by means of your neighbors."[22] Wisdom allows us to relate to our neighbors in such a loving and selfless way that we may act and speak with their true good in mind. Such love may appear as foolishness in the eyes of some, but will truly count as wisdom in the kingdom that we await with joyous expectation. In the end, Catherine is convinced that this is possible because we are made in the image of a trinitarian God. She prays,

> Then, when I considered myself in you, I saw that I am your image. You have gifted me with power from yourself, eternal Father, and my understanding with your wisdom—such wisdom as is proper to your only-begotten Son; and the Holy Spirit, who proceeds from you and from your Son, has given me a will, and so I am able to love.[23]

Catherine's life and work provide incentive to us to contemplate the loving face of Wisdom and to see ourselves reflected in God's wise face. With Catherine, we can invoke the Spirit to bestow on us the gift of wisdom that we might give God, ourselves, others and the world their due. If she were here today, no doubt Catherine would desire for us, as she did for her friends, that our knowledge of the truth be suffused with love so that we might offer as a blessing to those we hold dear a sage word of truth, freedom and love.

For Reflection

- *Who are the "wisdom figures" in your life? What makes them wisdom figures for you? Have you ever told them that they are wise? Have you ever thanked them?*

- *Western society has a tendency to keep knowledge and love in separate compartments. Has this been your experience? In what arenas of your life would you like to bring them together?*

- *Is Wisdom a name that you easily give to God? Why or why not?*

- *Spend some prayer time addressing the God who is Wisdom. The Christ who is Wisdom. The Holy Spirit who breathes the Wisdom of Christ into our lives.*

Closing Prayer

We close our retreat on a personal note, with Catherine's wishes for her friend, Bartolomeo Dominici, a Dominican who had been one of the first to join Catherine's circle of friends. Suzanne Noffke notes that he would later become one of her confessors and for the rest of her life one of her closest friends.

> I long to see fulfilled in you those words our Savior spoke to his disciples: "You are the light of the world and the salt of the earth" (Matthew 5:13-14). So with tremendous desire my soul longs for you to be such a son, so illumined by the light and warmth of the Holy Spirit, so seasoned with the salt of true knowledge and wisdom that you may zealously drive sin and demons from people's darkened souls. But I don't see how you can do this very well, or fulfill my desire, except by a constant burning love, and by conscientiously uniting yourself ever more closely with the true light and wisdom, fire and warmth, of divine charity, revealed to us in God's union with humanity.[24]

Notes

1 *Stories of the Spirit, Stories of the Heart: Parables of the Spiritual Path from Around the World*, p. 255.

2 *Letters*, p. 38.

3 Proverbs 8:1; 3b-4a; 5-7a; 8; 10-11; 17.

4 Raymond of Capua, pp. 1, 4, 6.

5 Raymond of Capua, p. 216.

6 Paul VI, quoted in *L'Osservatore Romano*, English edition (October 15, 1970), pp. 6, 7.

7 *Dialogue*, p. 155.

8 *Dialogue*, pp. 155-56.

9 *Letters*, p. 44.

10 1 Corinthians 13:1-3.

11 *Dialogue*, p. 36.

12 *Dialogue*, pp. 287, 290, 313.

13 *Dialogue*, pp. 49, 68, 136, 277.

14 *Dialogue*, p. 119.

15 *Dialogue*, p. 69.

16 *Dialogue*, p. 136.

17 *Dialogue*, p. 201.

18 *Dialogue*, p. 206.

19 1 Corinthians 2:7a, 10a, 11b.

20 Rahner, p. 17.

21 Rahner, p. 18.

22 *Dialogue*, p. 56.

23 *Dialogue*, p. 365.

24 *Letters*, p. 55.

Going Forth to Live the Theme

O eternal Trinity,
my sweet love!
You, light,
give us light.
You, wisdom,
give us wisdom.
You, supreme strength,
strengthen us.
Today, eternal God,
let our cloud be dissipated
so that we may perfectly know and follow your Truth
in truth,
with a free and simple heart.[1]

We come to the end of the journey into truth with
Catherine of Siena as our guide. She has taught us that
truth is not only an abstract, philosophical concept—
important as this is—but also a vibrant, challenging, ever-
developing experience and encounter with the God who
is Truth. The goal of such a retreat is to allow our reading,
reflection and prayer to affect our lives in meaningful
ways—truly to live and love in the truth in our everyday
lives.

Catherine has invited us to be truthful about
ourselves in all our sin and glory. We lose sight of these
truths when we give in to pseudo-values, to self-
deception, to "the great lie" that is a perversion of our
true humanness—that we are made to love others, to be
like God and with God.[2] We have many aids to help us.
Besides our faith, our friends, our families and the

Scriptures, we have the benefit of scientific and psychological knowledge unavailable to the Middle Ages. We have seen how Catherine did not exempt herself from this demand for self-knowledge. Scholar Suzanne Noffke challenges us to leave aside the "whitewashed" version of Catherine in order to see her as she was, in all her flaws and failures as well as in her courage and saintliness.[3] Raymond of Capua, Catherine's disciple and spiritual director, records her words of chastisement to him when she perceived that he was too adulatory or "easy" on her: "Oh, Lord God, what kind of spiritual father is this you have given me, who finds excuses for my sins!"[4] She wanted those around her to be truthful about who she was rather than to see her as an idol of perfection that she knew was false.

Catherine's passion for the truth should also lead us to the well—to the primary sources that have come down to us. One does not have to be a Catherine scholar to pick up her letters or her prayers or to read sections of her *Dialogue* in order to discover Catherine in her own words. She would want us to trust ourselves, not only to read *about* her but to reflect on her words themselves in order to discover there the truth that was hers in the fourteenth century and a piece of the truth that is ours today.

Our retreat director beckons us to our own wisdom, to our own concrete living out of the truth in love. For as we have seen, truth for Catherine was inseparable from love. Her writings are filled with this conviction. "If you are not found to be a *lover* of truth, you will never get to know the truth."[5] Indeed, she wants us to be lovers and spouses of Truth.[6] Few of us share Catherine's lifestyle, and we are certainly living in a time and place that are dramatically different from hers. This makes it all the more important to live our own lives with care and reflection and to look at *our* world with a long, loving, contemplative gaze. Catherine entered into the "nitty-gritty" of her chaotic and troubled world and we can ask no less of ourselves. This commitment to others was evident in her criticism of hermits who clung to their solitude when their presence was needed in the world. She wrote, "Now really, one's hold on the spiritual life is quite light if it is lost by moving! Apparently God is partial about location, and can be found only in the woods and nowhere else, even though there is need!"[7] The ironic humor of Catherine's words calls out to us some six hundred years later.

For the final truth about God and about ourselves is that we are called to lay down our lives for the other. We do this not "in the woods," but in the warp and woof of daily existence, in our homes, our workplaces, our neighborhoods, our country, our world. Our model is the God Catherine named Truth—the God who is madly in love with us, who sent the Son to give up his life in love, and sent us the fire of the Holy Spirit so that we might live in the truth that makes us free. As Christians, this is the truth that will keep us honest about ourselves, enable us to choose wisely between good and evil, and offer to others the fruits of our freedom and wisdom. At the beginning of Lent in 1379, a year before Catherine's death, she wrote a prayer, at the end of which she recommends her friends and disciples to God. Let us imagine that we are among that group for whom Catherine prays,

> I commend to you my children
> whom you have put on my shoulders.
> You commissioned me to keep them awake—
> me, who am always sleeping!
> Wake them up yourself,
> kind and compassionate God,
> so that the eyes of their understanding

may always be wide awake
in you.[8]

Notes

[1] *Prayers*, p. 105.

[2] Noffke, *Catherine of Siena: Vision Through a Distant Eye*, p. 16.

[3] Suzanne Noffke, "Demythologizing Catherine: The Wealth of Internal Evidence," *Spirituality Today* 32/1 (March 1980), pp. 4-12.

[4] Raymond of Capua. *The Life of St. Catherine*, p. 38. Cited in "Demythologizing Catherine," pp. 5-6.

[5] Letter 102 to Raymond of Capua. Cited in Noffke, p. 17.

[6] Letter 63 to Matteo Cenni. Cited in Noffke, p. 17.

[7] Letter 328. Cited in "Demythologizing Catherine," p. 10.

[8] *Prayers*, p. 136.

Deepening Your Acquaintance

Catherine's Writings

The Dialogue. Trans. Suzanne Noffke. New York: Paulist Press, 1980.

The Letters of St. Catherine of Siena. Vol. 1. Trans. Suzanne Noffke. Binghamton, N.Y.: Center for Medieval and Early Renaissance Studies, 1988.

The Prayers of Catherine of Siena. Ed. Suzanne Noffke. New York: Paulist Press, 1983.

Catherine of Siena: Passion for the Truth, Compassion for Humanity. Commentary by Mary O'Driscoll. New Rochelle, N.Y.: New City, 1993.

Books About Catherine

Fatula, Mary Ann. *Catherine of Siena's Way*. Wilmington, Del.: Michael Glazier, 1987.

Meade, Catherine M. *My Nature is Fire: Saint Catherine of Siena*. New York: Alba, 1991.

Noffke, Suzanne. *Catherine of Siena: Vision Through a Distant Eye*. Collegeville, Minn.: The Liturgical Press, 1996. [Includes comprehensive bibliography of works in English.]

Raymond of Capua. *The Life of Catherine of Siena*. Trans. Conleth Kearns. Wilmington, Del.: Michael Glazier, 1980.

Undset, Sigrid. *Catherine of Siena*. Trans. Kate Austin-Lund. New York: Sheed & Ward, 1954.

Articles and Chapters About Catherine

Ashley, Benedict. "St. Catherine of Siena's Principles of Spiritual Direction." *Spirituality Today* 33 (March 1981), pp. 43-52.

Fatula, Mary Ann. "The Holy Spirit Hidden in the Experience of Human Weakness." *Spirituality Today* 36 (Summer 1984), pp. 109-122.

Foley, Nadine. "Catherine of Siena's Wisdom and Spirituality." *Spirituality Today* (1993), pp. 205-19.

Galligan, Sheila. "Sheltered by the Mercy: St. Catherine's Gentle Way." *Spirituality Today* 42 (Spring 1990), pp. 15-36.

Giles, Mary E. "The Feminist Mystic." In *The Feminist Mystic and Other Essays on Women and Spirituality*, ed. Mary E. Giles. New York: Crossroad Publishing Co., 1982.

Kearns, Conleth. "The Wisdom of Saint Catherine." *Angelicum* 57 (1980), pp. 324-43.

McLaughlin, Eleanor. "Women, Power, and the Pursuit of Holiness in Medieval Christianity." In *Women of Spirit*, ed. Rosemary Ruether and Eleanor McLaughlin. New York: Simon & Schuster, 1979, pp. 100-130.

McNamara, William. "A Model for the Twentieth Century: Catherine of Siena." *Sisters Today* 52 (April 1980), pp. 195-99.

O'Driscoll, Mary. "Catherine the Theologian." *Spirituality Today* 40 (Spring 1988), pp. 4-17.

Schneiders, Sandra M. "Spiritual Discernment in the *Dialogue* of Saint Catherine of Siena." *Horizons* (Spring 1982), pp. 47-59.

Spirituality Today 32/1 (March 1980). This entire issue is devoted to Catherine of Siena, with articles by Suzanne Noffke, Jeremy Finnegan, Marie Walter Flood, Mary O'Driscoll, Marie Stephen Reges.